HAWAI`I VOLCANO WATCH

HAWAI'I VOLCANO WATCH

A Pictorial History, 1779–1991

THOMAS L. WRIGHT

TAEKO JANE TAKAHASHI

J. D. GRIGGS

University of Hawaii Press

and

Hawaii Natural History Association

Printed in Singapore

97 96 95 94 93 92 5 4 3 2 1

Jacket/Cover: Lava from the Pu'u 'Ō'ō-Kūpaianaha eruption covers new black sand beach east of Kupapa'u Point on the eastern boundary of Hawaii Volcanoes National Park (USGS photo by J. D. Griggs, 2/17/88).

Library of Congress Cataloging-in-Publication Data

Wright. Thomas L. (Thomas Llewellyn), 1935–

Hawai'i volcano watch : a pictorial history. 1779–1991

/ Thomas L. Wright, Taeko Jane Takahashi, J. D. Griggs.

p.   cm.

"An expanded version of a public lecture entitled '200 years of volcano watching in Hawai'i' delivered by the first author at the opening of the Smithsonian Institution exhibition 'Inside active volcanoes' in 1989, and subsequently at other museums..." — P.

Includes bibliographical references (p.   ) and index.

ISBN 0–8248–1439–8 (cloth). — ISBN 0–8248–1478–9 (pbk.)

1. Volcanoes—Hawaii—History. 2. Volcanoes—Hawaii—History—Pictorial works. I. Takahashi, Taeko Jane, 1941–   II. Griggs, J. D., 1941–   III. Title.

QE524.W75   1992

551.2'1'09969—dc20   92–16592

CIP

Book design by Marquand Books, Inc.

This book is affectionately dedicated to our

colleagues at the Hawaiian Volcano Observatory

— past, present, and future

CONTENTS

ACKNOWLEDGMENTS

We acknowledge the help of the following organizations for their assistance in providing illustrations: Bernice P. Bishop Museum, Honolulu; Thomas H. Hamilton Library, University of Hawaii at Manoa; Hawaii Volcanoes National Park; Hawaiian Historical Society, Honolulu; Hawaiian Mission Children's Society Library, Honolulu; Lyman House Memorial Museum, Hilo; Maui Historical Society. Photo credits to individuals are given in the figure captions.

Dorothy Barrère, Russ Apple, and Bob Koyanagi checked the manuscript and figure captions for historical accuracy. Frank Trusdell helped produce computer-assisted graphic illustrations. The final manuscript benefited from reviews by R. I. Tilling, P. W. Lipman, and J. P. Lockwood of the U.S. Geological Survey, and two anonymous reviewers. We thank the staff of the University of Hawaii Press for their cooperation and encouragement during the preparation of this book.

PREFACE

Volcanic activity has captured the imagination of everyone who has ever lived in or visited Hawai'i, beginning with the Hawaiians themselves, who incorporated their respect for volcanoes into legends and chants about the volcano goddess Pele. In early Western exploration, from Captain Cook's voyage, through the journeys of Christian missionaries and the travels of artists and writers, to early scientific excursions, such as the famous U.S. Exploring Expedition, visitors to Hawai'i regarded the volcanoes as fascinating natural phenomena.

This book is an expanded version of a public lecture entitled "200 Years of Volcano Watching in Hawai'i," delivered by the first author at the opening of the Smithsonian Institution exhibition "Inside Active Volcanoes" in 1989 and subsequently at other museums, historical societies, and scientific institutions both within and outside Hawai'i. The lecture was based on research for an annotated bibliography of observations on Hawaiian volcanic activity (Wright and Takahashi, 1989).

This pictorial history provides a sampling of the written observations, insightful interpretations, and spectacular illustrations of volcanic activity in Hawai'i during the past two centuries. We cover primarily the era before sophisticated instrumentation, when interpretations of volcanic phenomena were made from careful, firsthand observations of eruptions. We deal briefly with the modern era—in which visual observations are supplemented and quantified by extensive use of sensitive instruments — by emphasizing the relationship of modern observations and interpretations to the vision or insight of earlier observers. The book closes with a perspective on living with active volcanoes. This perspective was an integral part of the Hawaiian's daily life and philosophy, but it has become more alien in a world whose functions are increasingly detached from nature and where acceptance of natural processes is replaced by attempts to control nature.

INTRODUCTION

Near the close of the dinosaurs' reign on land and before the first whales appeared in the sea, lava leaked onto the floor of the Pacific Ocean near the present site of the island of Hawai`i. Thus was born the first Hawaiian volcano. Over the next 70 million years or so, more than 100 such small fields of lava grew by repeated eruptions until they reached the ocean surface to become large volcanic islands (fig. 1). Then, in time, these islands were destroyed by subsidence and erosion as the Pacific plate moved northwestward, away from the Hawaiian "hotspot," or fixed source of magma in the Earth's mantle.

The Hawaiian Islands, extending from Kaua`i in the northwest to Hawai`i in the southeast (fig. 2), illustrate different stages in this process of island birth, growth, and death. One kilometer below sea level, to the south of the island of Hawai`i, the newest

Hawaiian volcano, Lō`ihi seamount, is gradually making its way to the surface (fig. 3A). Hawai`i's two highest volcanoes, Mauna Loa (fig. 3B) and Mauna Kea (fig. 3C), represent the principal stages of volcanic growth. At the other end of the chain, scattered cones and tuff rings on Kaua`i and O`ahu (fig. 3D), including the famous landmark Diamond Head, represent the last stage in the construction of a Hawaiian volcano.

The processes of decay begin while the volcanoes are still growing. The effects of erosion are visible in the steeply incised windward coasts of all the islands and in submarine canyons extending far from shore. Some volcanoes have lost part of their flanks in gigantic landslides, which cover extensive areas on the ocean bottom surrounding the islands (fig. 4). Even without the catastrophic collapses, the great weight of a volcano causes it to sink into the ocean floor at up to half the rate at which it is built. The subsidence history is marked by submarine terraces surrounding each island in the chain. The combined processes of degradation result in eventual resubmergence of the volcanoes beneath the ocean. From the summit of Mauna Loa, through tiny Niʻihau Island, to the distant Aleutian trench, the Hawaiian-Emperor Chain traces the growth of giant volcanoes and their subsequent reduction to coral-covered seamounts.

The island of Hawaiʻi holds an important key to understanding the birth and death of Hawaiian volcanoes because we can directly observe and study the activity of Kīlauea, Mauna Loa, and Hualālai (see table 1 in the Appendix). The Hawaiians recognized the islands they lived on as volcanic and incorporated their understanding of volcanic processes into legends chronicling the travels and behavior of the volcano goddess Pele (fig. 5). The early Western explorers also inferred the volcanic nature of the islands, but saw no activity. Beginning in 1820, Christian missionaries arrived and recorded their own observations, as well as those of the Hawaiians, previously preserved only through native chants and legends. Nineteenth-century scientists brought yet another perspective to the study of Hawaiʻi's active volcanoes through their records of observations published in books and monographs by the end of the first decade of the twentieth century. These scientific treatises provided a strong foundation for the more detailed studies of the succeeding decades.

The twentieth century saw the establishment of the Hawaiian Volcano Observatory and the beginning of systematic monitoring and dedicated scientific study of the volcanoes. Modern study of the volcanoes, in which visual observations are augmented by measurements using sophisticated scientific instruments, has generated hypotheses that can be tested against a global understanding of volcanic processes. This book traces the history of volcano observation in Hawaiʻi, emphasizing several themes: (1) the value of the early observations by Hawaiians, missionaries, and scientists; (2) the history of more systematic observations by scientists, particularly those associated with the first years of the Hawaiian Volcano Observatory; (3) the evolution of ideas about Hawaiian volcanic processes, comparing what we can quantify from modern instrumental monitoring and continuous observation during the past several decades with interpretations made in the nineteenth and early twentieth centuries, and (4) the challenge of living with active volcanoes—a way of life for the Hawaiians, whose perspective was appreciated anew when lava flows from Kīlauea's Puʻu ʻŌʻō-Kūpaianaha eruption covered the historic Kalapana area in 1990.

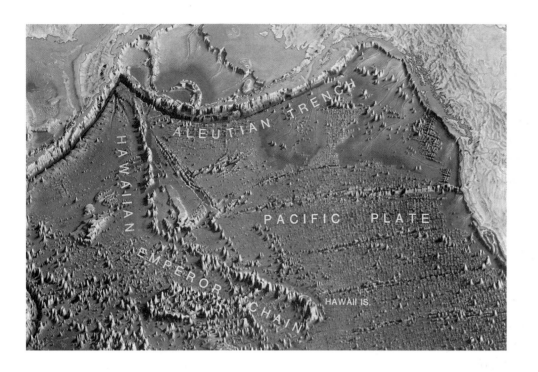

Figure 1. The Hawaiian-Emperor Chain of islands and seamounts lies entirely within the Pacific plate, which is currently moving northwest at a rate of more than 10 centimeters per year. The bend in the chain reflects a change in plate motion that occurred about 40 million years ago. The oldest part of the chain is being subducted at the Aleutian trench. The youngest part, centered on the island of Hawai`i, lies directly over a "hot spot" in the Earth's mantle that has remained stationary for more than 70 million years (modified after Heezen and Tharp, 1977; used with permission).

Figure 2. The Hawaiian Islands from Kaua`i *(upper left)* to Hawai`i *(lower right)*. The island of Hawai`i lies directly over a "hot spot" in the Earth's mantle within which rock is heated and melted to form magma. Early lava flows from the Pu`u `Ō`ō-Kūpaianaha eruption of Kīlauea Volcano are shown in red. Lō`ihi seamount, also active at the leading edge of the hot spot, lies under 1 kilometer of water just south of the island of Hawai`i (Dynamic Graphics, 1984; bathymetric contour interval 1,000 meters, vertical exaggeration 6X; used with permission).

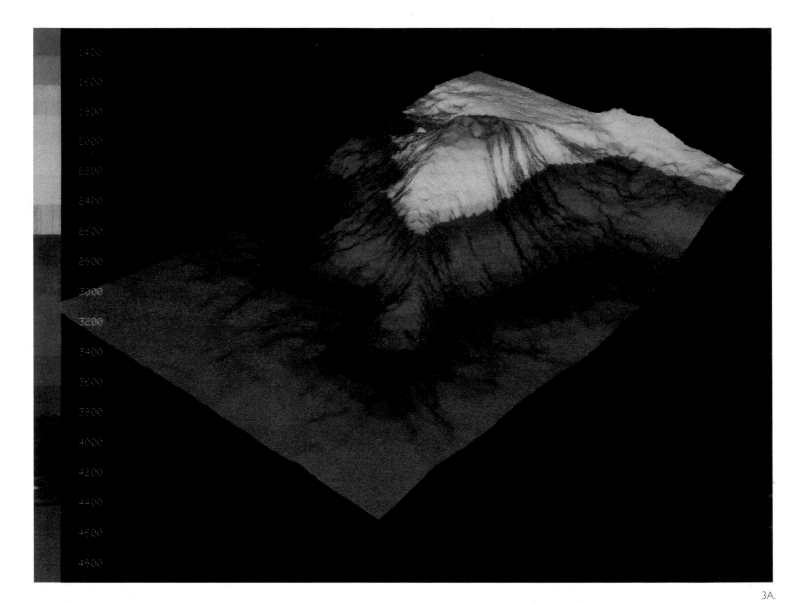

3A.

Figure 3. The stages of Hawaiian volcanism. **A**, a computer-drawn perspective model of Lō`ihi seamount, now in the earliest, or *pre-shield,* stage of activity, using SEA BEAM bathymetric data (Fornari et al. 1988, p. 15, 232). **B**, Mauna Loa, whose broad profile illustrates the voluminous *shield* stage of activity when the volcano lies directly over the hot spot. The smooth and shallow profile results from the accumulation of thin, very fluid basaltic lava flows. The term shield refers to its shape, which resembles an inverted warrior's shield (USGS photo by T. J. Takahashi, 10/91). **C**, Mauna Kea. The irregular profile is due to the abundance of steep-sided cinder cones formed by eruption of andesite, less fluid and more explosive than the basalt that characterizes the shield stage. The steepness of Mauna Kea's upper slopes also reflects the greater viscosity (lower fluidity) of lava in the waning, or *post-shield,* stage of activity as the volcano moves off the hot spot. Remnants of the earlier shield stage are shown by the shallow, sloping surface at the *right* (USGS photo by T. J. Takahashi, 10/91.) **D**,tuff cones with central craters represent the final, or "rejuvenated," stage of Hawaiian volcanism. Cones like this are formed long after the volcano has moved off the hot spot. Aerial photo taken off Koko Head, Oahu (photo courtesy of Camera Hawaii; used with permission).

3B.

3C.

3D.

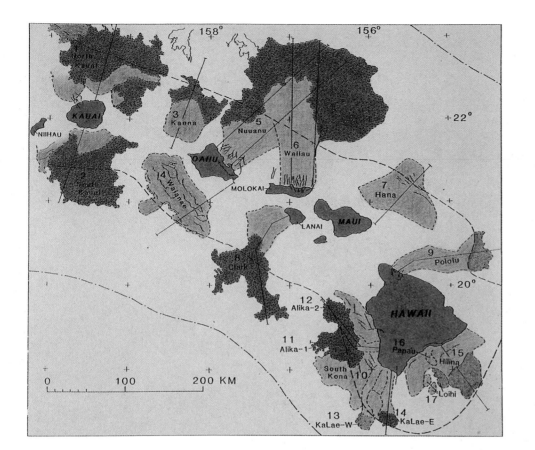

Figure 4. Aprons of landslide debris, mapped by recent deep-water sidescan sonar (GLORIA) surveys, surround the Hawaiian Islands and attest to the inherent instability of volcanoes built largely under water. The islands are shown in *green*. Massive submarine slumps are shown in *light brown* and the hummocky ground at the distal end of large landslides (*debris avalanches*) in *dark brown,* illustrating catastrophic loss by landsliding of parts of the volcanoes (modified after Moore et al., 1989, p. 17,467).

Figure 5. The line of smoke traces Pele's travels down the Hawaiian Chain from the extinct volcanoes on Kaua`i (*upper left*) to her current home at Kīlauea on the island of Hawai`i (*lower right*). Original drawing by Lisa Koyanagi, 2/92 (used with permission).

Figure 6. Polynesian voyagers are greeted by erupting volcanoes as they approach the island of Hawai`i. Painting, "The Discovery of Hawai`i—Polynesian Voyagers before 450 A.D.," by H. K. Kane, 1986 (used with permission).

DISCOVERY AND EARLY EXPLORATION OF THE ACTIVE VOLCANOES

The islands were settled by Polynesians as early as A.D. 300 (fig. 6). Captain James Cook, who discovered the islands for the West in 1778, first visited the island of Hawai'i a year later, coming ashore at Kealakekua Bay (fig. 7). He wrote: "Owyhee has every appearance in nature to suppose it once to have been a vulcano ... The eastern side of the island is one continued bed of lava from the summit to the sea, and under the sea in 50 fathom water some distance from the shore..." (Ledyard, 1783, p. 123). His crew saw no actual volcanic activity, but did make a map (fig. 8). They attempted to climb Mauna Loa, underestimating the distance and difficulty of ascent, and turned back before reaching the timberline.

Captain George Vancouver, during his cruises of 1792–1794, was the next explorer to come ashore at Kealakekua Bay. Another map was made, differing little from Cook's. Vancouver and his crew also saw no volcanic activity. The maps by Cook and Vancouver do not recognize Kīlauea, even though it had been active, as recently as 1790, with lava flows on the east rift zone and an explosive eruption at Kīlauea's summit. A botanist on Vancouver's cruise, Archibald Menzies, made the first successful ascent of Mauna Loa in February 1794. Menzies estimated the heights of Mauna Loa and Mauna Kea within 100 feet (31 meters) of the currently accepted value, a remarkable surveying feat for that time. In January of the same year, he made the first ascent of Hualālai (fig. 9), the third active volcano on the island. Hualālai erupted in 1800 and 1801, a few years after Vancouver's visits.

Eight years before Vancouver landed at Kealakekua Bay, the French explorer Jean François de Galaup de la Pérouse had visited the islands. Although La Pérouse did not visit the island of Hawai'i, he made excellent maps of the other Hawaiian islands. La Pérouse's map of the island of Maui was more important geologically than he could have realized, because where his map had shown a bay (fig. 10), Vancouver's map showed an extra spit of land. In 1879 Lorrin Thurston, Hawai'i statesman and publisher of two of Honolulu's newspapers, visited Maui, where he was told about a lava flow into La Pérouse Bay that was seen by relatives of living Hawaiians (Thurston, 1924). Using 33 years as the average span of a Hawaiian generation, Thurston had calculated the date of this flow as about 1750. In 1942 geologists Harold Stearns and Gordon Macdonald outlined the flow on a map showing that the eruption took place at two vents, the lower of which fed the flow that nearly fills La Pérouse Bay (fig. 11). In 1965 B. L. Ootsdam examined the original maps of La Pérouse and Vancouver and was able to demonstrate, by comparing the two, that the lava flow described by Thurston and by Stearns and Macdonald was in exactly the place where the maps were discrepant, and thus he could confidently infer that lava had reached the ocean between 1786 and 1794.

Other early explorers passed by the island of Hawai'i, but none landed. Some of these cruises reported volcanic activity, seen from a great distance. The reports are vague, and the dates do not jibe with later second- or thirdhand reports from observers on land. No firsthand observations of eruptions were written down until almost three decades after the departure of Vancouver's ships.

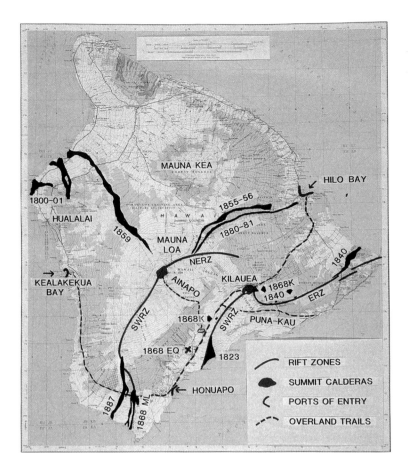

Figure 7. Ports of entry and trails used in the early exploration of the island of Hawai'i. The first Western explorers came ashore at Kealakekua Bay. Some of those who came later landed either at Hilo Bay or at Honu'apo. Loci of eruptions (shown in red) are the summits of Kīlauea and Mauna Loa and two rift zones radiating outward from the summit of each volcano. A few of the lava flows erupted in the nineteenth century are shown in black, including those from eruptions of Hualālai. The epicenter of the great earthquake of 1868 is marked as a large, red X. Travelers to Kīlauea from the west came up the southwest rift zone (SWRZ) to the summit, while those from Hilo used a trail that was close to the present Hilo–Volcano road. The summit caldera of Mauna Loa was approached from the south along the 'Ainapō Trail, heading up from what is now Kapāpala Ranch. Observers of eruptions on Mauna Loa's northeast rift zone (NERZ) took the difficult route from Hilo, up the Wailuku River toward the saddle separating Mauna Kea and Mauna Loa, thence to the rift and summit (USGS base map).

Figure 8. The first map of the island of Hawai'i, made in 1779 by Henry Roberts, a member of Captain Cook's crew. Four volcanoes are shown, and only the two largest ones are named. Kīlauea is conspicuously absent from this map and from a similar one made following Vancouver's voyages of 1792–1794. Neither Cook nor Vancouver visited the eastern side of Hawai'i or saw any volcanic activity (Fitzpatrick, 1986, p. 17).

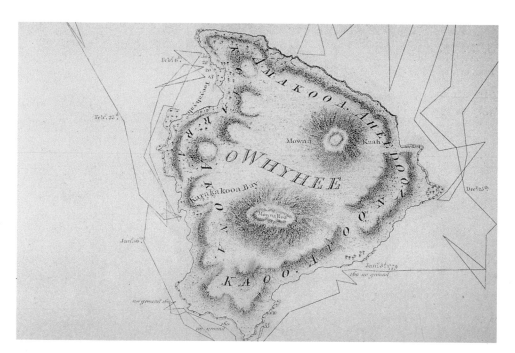

Figure 9. The summit of Hualālai Volcano at the time of the first ascent by Archibald Menzies in 1794 (Anderson, 1960, plate following p. 148).

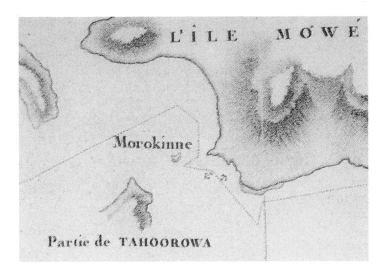

10A.

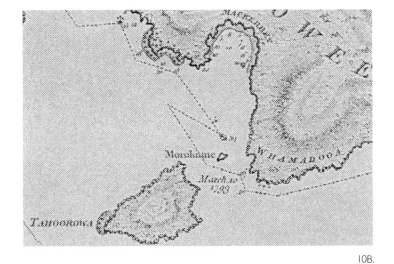

10B.

Figure 10. Enlarged portions of two early maps of the island of Maui. **A**, voyage of La Pérouse in 1786 (Fitzpatrick, 1986, p. 29). **B**, voyage of Vancouver in 1794. Note the difference in the southwestern coastline. Part of the bay shown by La Pérouse (later named for him) is shown here as a spit of land. This difference was used later to infer a 1790 date for an eruption of Haleakalā volcano (Fitzpatrick, 1986, p. 41).

Figure 11. The 1790 flow from Haleakalā. Note how the lava that went into the sea explains the discrepancy between the two maps in the preceding figure (Macdonald et al., 1983, p. 58).

A MODERN UNDERSTANDING OF KĪLAUEA VOLCANO

The significance of early work in Hawai'i can be appreciated through a brief summary of our modern understanding of the plumbing of Kīlauea Volcano (fig. 12), gained from more than 30 years of instrumental monitoring by the U.S. Geological Survey's Hawaiian Volcano Observatory. Magma rises from deep in the Earth to a shallow storage zone beneath Kīlauea's summit, from which it erupts to the surface at the summit or on a rift zone (see fig. 7), or moves underground as intrusions. Before an eruption, while the chamber is being filled, the summit expands or inflates (fig. 13). During eruption or intrusion on the rift zone, the summit subsides again in response to withdrawal of magma.

To a remarkable degree, this general process was understood by the Hawaiians, who associated dying of the fires in Halema'uma'u with eruption on the flanks, the lava traveling from the summit to the shore via an underground passage. The connection between summit collapse and rift eruption was also correctly inferred by the missionary William Ellis, as well as by James D. Dana and later scientists.

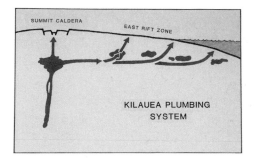

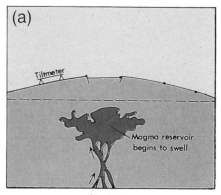

Figure 12. Cross-section of Kīlauea's plumbing system, drawn parallel to the east rift zone. Magma rising from the Earth's mantle, and destined to erupt anywhere on the volcano, is first stored in a holding reservoir beneath Kīlauea's summit. Arrows show eruptions occurring at Kīlauea's summit or at various points along the rift zone, including its undersea extension. Red patches show magma left underground as *intrusions*, estimated by modern workers to be more than half of all magma supplied to the volcano (Dzurisin et al., 1984). During some eruptions (e.g., that of Kīlauea in 1840, as described by both Coan and Wilkes) vents migrate up or down the rift zone (modified after Wright and Fiske, 1971).

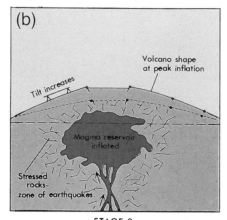

STAGE 1
INFLATION BEGINS

STAGE 2
INFLATION AT PEAK

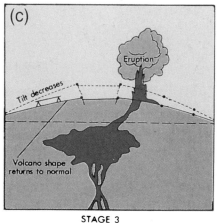

STAGE 3
ERUPTION-DEFLATION

Figure 13. The surface of the volcano changes shape prior to, and following, an eruption. When Kīlauea was continuously active in its summit caldera, the draining of lava from Halema'uma'u Crater was correctly interpreted by early observers to presage rift, or even offshore, eruption (Heliker et al., 1986, p. 18).

EXPLORERS, MISSIONARIES, AND NINETEENTH-CENTURY SCIENTISTS

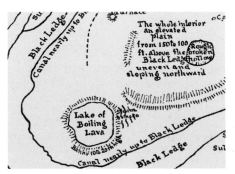

Kīlauea, Hawai'i's most frequently active volcano, was first visited in 1823 by a group of Christian missionaries led by William Ellis (fig. 14; Ellis, 1825). Ellis, a London missionary working in Tahiti, was recruited to lead a trip around the island of Hawai'i because he was fluent in the Hawaiian language. His party traveled along the southeast side of the island (fig. 15) just after an eruption had occurred in the Kapāpala district (fig. 16) on Kīlauea's southwest rift zone. He then visited Kīlauea's summit caldera, where he found an active lava lake containing many conical vents (fig. 17). Ellis' map of the island (fig. 18) for the first time recognized Kīlauea, although it otherwise differed little from Vancouver's earlier one.

Ellis not only made astute observations but also learned much about Kīlauea's eruptions from Hawaiians, who told him about an explosive eruption originating at the volcano's summit some 30 years earlier. This eruption destroyed part of a Hawaiian army (fig. 19) whose footprints were preserved in the ash that covered the desert south of Hale-ma'uma'u. Sheldon Dibble, a missionary who arrived a decade later, transcribed an oral account of this tragic event:

> The army of Keoua set out on their way in three different companies. The company in advance had not proceeded far before the ground began to shake and rock beneath their feet and it became quite impossible to stand. Soon a dense cloud of darkness was seen to rise out of the crater, and almost at the same instant the electrical effect upon the air was so great that the thunder began to roar in the heavens and the lightning to flash. It continued to ascend and spread abroad until the whole region was enveloped and the light of day was entirely excluded. The

darkness was the more terrific, being made visible by an awful glare from streams of red and blue light variously combined that issued from the pit below, and being lit up at intervals by the intense flashes of lightning from above. Soon followed an immense volume of sand and cinders which were thrown in high heaven and came down in a destructive shower for many miles around. Some few persons of the forward company were burned to death by the sand and cinders and others were seriously injured. All experienced a suffocating sensation upon the lungs and hastened on with all possible speed.

The rear body, which was nearest the volcano at the time of the eruption, seemed to suffer the least injury, and after the earthquake and shower of sand had passed over, hastened forward. . . . But . . . on coming up to their comrades of the center party, they discovered them all to have become corpses. Some were lying down, and others sitting upright clasping with dying grasp their wives and children and joining noses . . . as in the act of taking final leave. So much like life they looked that they at first supposed them merely at rest, and it was not until they had come up to them and handled them that they could detect their mistake. The whole party, including women and children, not one of them survived to relate the catastrophe that had befallen their comrades. The only living being they found was a solitary hog. (Dibble, 1843, p. 52)

This remarkable account, combined with modern study of the 1790 ash deposits (fig. 20), indicates that a blast of hot, ash-poor gas (*base surge*) killed the Hawaiian soldiers, sparing those not in its direct path (Swanson and Christiansen, 1973).

Ellis continued his journey, traveling from Kīlauea's summit, down Hawaiian trails (fig. 21) to the ocean at Kealakomo (fig. 22), where he learned how the eruption he had just missed had devastated the southern part of Kapāpala. His party then traversed the southeast coast, visiting Waha'ula heiau (fig. 23) and Hawaiian villages at Kapa'ahu (fig. 24), Kalapana, and Kaimū (fig. 25), before passing the east cape of the island (fig. 26) on their return to Hilo.

Ellis' party was treated royally when they arrived at Kaimū, as it was a homecoming for Ellis' Hawaiian guide Mauae. Here Ellis was told that the Kaimū district was last inundated by lava during the reign of Alapa'i in the first half of the eighteenth century. He also was shown ground cracks that opened during a severe earthquake two months before his arrival. The cracks and the descriptions of seawater entering an inland water well testify to a violent lateral movement and subsidence of land similar to what happened in November 1975 in the same area (fig. 27; Tilling et al., 1976).

Ellis' reports of conversations with native people reveal the remarkable insights the Hawaiians had into the volcanic processes in Hawai'i, woven as they were into the fabric of legends regarding the travels of the volcano goddess Pele and her behavior at Kīlauea. For example, Hawaiian legends trace Pele's travels from the island of Kaua'i to her final home in Kīlauea's Halema'uma'u Crater (fig. 5; Westerveldt, 1916), evidence that the Hawaiians recognized the progressively increasing age of the volcanoes to the northwest.

Two years after Ellis' pioneering trip, Lord George Byron landed at Hilo Bay with a group of scientists (Byron, 1826) who produced the first map of Kīlauea's summit caldera (fig. 28). They camped on the isthmus that separates Kīlauea Iki Crater from the main caldera. In 1832 Kīlauea erupted on "Byron's Ledge," sending lava into both the caldera and the crater, destroying all evidence of Byron's camp.

In 1840 and 1841, the U.S. Exploring Expedition, led by Lieutenant Charles Wilkes (fig. 29), arrived at Hilo Bay with a large and varied party of scientists. The U.S. Ex. Ex., as it was termed, was charged with mapping and charting little-known regions of the Pacific and southern oceans, advancing the diplo-

Figure 14. William Ellis, an English missionary, who came to the "Sandwich Islands" from Tahiti in 1822. In 1823 he was asked to lead a group of American missionaries, including Asa Thurston, Charles Stewart, Artemis Bishop, and Joseph Goodrich, to the island of Hawai'i in order to evaluate the prospects of establishing missions on the island (Hawaiian Mission Children's Society, 1969, p. 88).

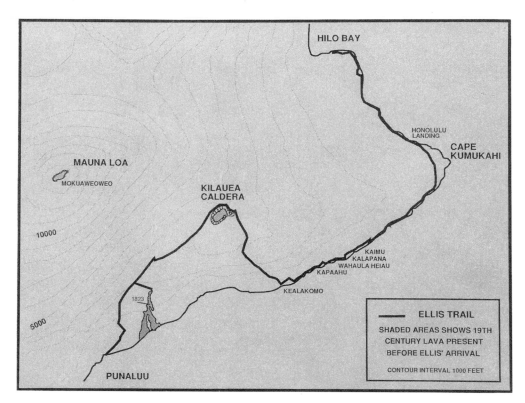

Figure 15. Ellis' route at Kīlauea. The 1823 lava was erupted just prior to Ellis' visit. Much of his route along the southeast coastline has been covered by new lava, including land still being covered in 1991 by the Pu'u 'Ō'ō-Kūpaianaha eruption of Kīlauea (see fig. 140B) (computer-assisted drawing adapted from USGS base maps).

Figure 16. "The Burning Chasms at Ponahohoa," visited by Ellis on his trip from Kealakekua Bay to Kīlauea's summit. The chasms lie on Kīlauea's southwest rift zone at the upper end of the "great crack," source fissure of the 1823 eruption that had just ended. This fanciful drawing depicts a rift depression (graben), possibly formed during a large earthquake several months before Ellis' arrival. Steam rises from the recently active vents of the 1823 eruption (Ellis, 1825, plate following p. 208 [1827 edition]; courtesy of Bishop Museum).

Figure 17. Kīlauea caldera at the time of Ellis' visit in 1823. The prominent shelf separating the inner pit of Halemaʻumaʻu from the rest of the caldera was termed the black ledge. This drawing is not as fanciful as it seems. The smoking chimneys, drawn as sharp cones, resemble spatter vents observed and photographed in later eruptions (see figs. 52B, 109) (Ellis, 1825, plate facing p. 226 [1827 edition]; courtesy of Bishop Museum).

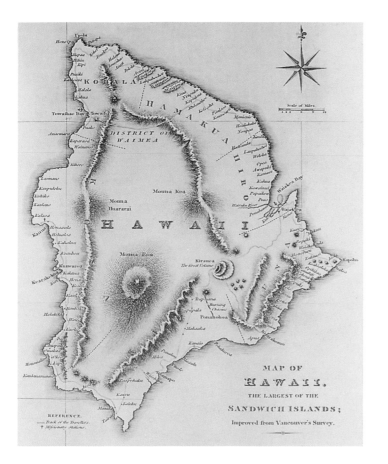

Figure 19. Part of the army of the Hawaiian chieftain Keōua after the 1790 eruption of Kīlauea. Painting by P. Rockwood, 1950s. Death was apparently by asphyxiation from hot, ash-laden gases produced in a lateral blast similar to, but much smaller than, the blast at Mount St. Helens in May 1980 (Swanson and Christiansen, 1973). It is likely that much of the present Kīlauea caldera was formed during the series of explosions that culminated in the 1790 blast. Ash from the 1790 eruption extends more than 20 kilometers away from Kīlauea's summit. This eruption demonstrates the explosive potential of Kīlauea, normally thought of as a gentle volcano presenting little hazard to human life. The footprints depicted in the painting can be seen in the ash deposits of the Ka'ū desert in Hawaii Volcanoes National Park (courtesy of Hawaii Volcanoes National Park).

Figure 18. Map of Hawai'i made following Ellis' visit. "Kirauea, The Great Volcano," is now prominent as the fifth volcano on the island. Hualālai ("Mount Huararai") is shown at left center. The present-day town of Hilo is labeled "Waiakea." Ellis' route from "Kearakekua" (Kealakekua Bay) to Hilo via Kīlauea's southwest rift zone, summit, and Puna coast, is shown as a faint double line (Fitzpatrick, 1986, p. 86).

Figure 20. Section of Keanakāko'i ash deposited from the 1790 series of eruptions at Kīlauea's summit. Undulating and cross-laminated layers, typical of base-surge deposits, were emplaced during the blast that killed Keōua's warriors (Swanson and Christiansen, 1973, p. 84).

Figure 21. Hawaiian trail leading to a "meeting place,"
southeast Kīlauea coast (Emory et al., 1965, plate I.B)
(photo 7/26/64, courtesy of Bishop Museum).

Figure 22. Hawaiian homesite at Kealakomo on the southeast coast of Hawai'i. Kealakomo was covered by lava from the Mauna Ulu eruption of 1969–1974 (see fig. 140B) (photo by C. D. Smart, 7/26/64, courtesy of Bishop Museum).

Figure 23. The *luakini* heiau at Wahaʻula. The heiau, used for human sacrifice as late as 1815, was built upon a low pali *(fault scarp)* overlooking the ocean. It now stands surrounded and partly invaded by lava from Kīlauea's Puʻu ʻŌʻō-Kūpaianaha eruption (fig. 135) (photo by Ed Ladd, 10/67, courtesy of Hawaii Volcanoes National Park).

Figure 24. Hawaiian stone enclosures in the vicinity of Kapaʻahu, east of Wahaʻula and just outside Hawaii Volcanoes National Park. This area, subdivided for development in the late 1970s, is also covered by lava from Kīlauea's Puʻu ʻŌʻō-Kūpaianaha eruption (fig. 114) (photo courtesy of D. Hamilton, 2/64).

Figure 25. Kaimū Bay and black sand beach, circa 1926. The beach was formed in the eighteenth century when black sand derived from lava entering the ocean to the east was deposited by prevailing west-moving longshore currents. The beach and bay were completely obliterated in 1990 by lava from Kīlauea's Puʻu ʻŌʻō-Kūpaianaha eruption (fig. 137) (photo courtesy of Bishop Museum).

Figure 26. Hawaiian canoe sheds inland from Kapele Bay, north of Cape Kumukahi, between the 1840 and 1960 eruptions that covered part of Ellis' trail (fig. 140B) (photo courtesy of Bishop Museum).

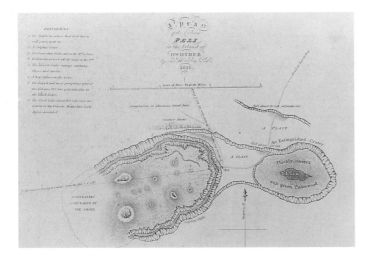

Figure 28. The first map of Kīlauea caldera, made by Lieutenant Malden during the visit of Lord Byron in 1825. Byron's party camped in the area labeled A PLAIN separating Kīlauea Iki Crater (right) from the main Kīlauea caldera. This area is now called Byron's Ledge. The depiction of a central, less-forested area in Kīlauea Iki is intriguing, suggesting the possibility of an otherwise unreported eruption, perhaps associated with the latter part of the activity that culminated in the 1790 explosive eruption (Fitzpatrick, 1986, p. 89).

Figure 27. A coconut grove at Halapē on Kīlauea's south coast, now under water because of coastal subsidence caused by the magnitude 7.2 earthquake of November 29, 1975. The resulting local tsunami killed two persons camping at Halapē. Hawaiian people on the Puna coast told Ellis about one or more large earthquakes a few months prior to his visit that had caused coastal subsidence and ground cracking not, apparently, as extensive as what occurred in 1975. The 1823 earthquakes were probably also responsible for the formation of the depression (graben) on Kīlauea's southwest rift zone depicted in fig. 16 (USGS photo by R.T. Holcomb, 12/4/75).

matic and commercial interests of the United States, and making scientific observations (Appleman, 1987). To achieve the latter goal, the expedition carried a corps of civilian scientists, foremost among whom was James D. Dana (fig. 30), later to become one of the giants of American geology. By the time of his arrival in Hawai'i, Dana had already published his comprehensive *System of Mineralogy;* he later became editor of the *American Journal of Science.* Wilkes' observations were published as a five-volume narrative (Wilkes, 1845). Dana's contributions to the geology of the Pacific Ocean Basin were published separately as Volume 10 of the scientific reports of the U.S. Ex. Ex. (Dana, 1849).

Due to peculiarities in the operations of the expedition, Dana himself spent little of his time on the island of Hawai'i (Appleman, 1987). Even so, Dana's contributions to understanding of the origin of the Hawaiian Islands were substantial, and for these he has been called America's first volcanologist. Dana correctly inferred the order of extinction of the volcanoes from northwest to southeast, but he believed incorrectly that all the volcanoes originated simultaneously from a single fissure that widened to the southeast to explain the greater activity at that end of the chain. J. P. Couthouy, the expedition's conchologist, wrote to Dana, offering an alternative explanation: "The foregoing observations are applied to the course of volcanic action at the islands taken separately, with a view to show that it has been successive in each, from the western to the southeastern extremity of the group, and the possibility that they were also forced up in regular succession by the subterranean fire" (Dana, 1849, p. 283, as quoted by Appleman, 1987, p. 1616).

It is interesting to note that the Hawaiians, like Couthouy, had deduced that the volcanoes were born *and* died in the same order, from Kaua'i to the currently active Kīlauea, in agreement with modern dating of the volcanoes (fig. 31).

Wilkes visited Kīlauea's summit, finding it much as Ellis had described. The Exploring Expedition's artist, Titian Peale, painted day- and night-time views of the lava lake in Kīlauea caldera (figs. 32, 33). Wilkes' crew also traversed the length of Kīlauea's east rift zone, having heard from the Hawaiians about an eruption that had taken place only months before their arrival. They produced a map of the 1840 eruption (fig. 34), which had progressed down the rift zone, ending with an entry of lava into the ocean. Remarkably, it was almost a century before any other eruption of Kīlauea was accurately mapped.

Wilkes and other members of the expedition followed their observations at Kīlauea with an ascent of Mauna Loa and produced the first map of Moku'āweoweo, Mauna Loa's summit caldera (fig. 35). The account of the troubles encountered in reaching the summit with a large party of natives, none of whom were acclimated to other than the subtropical conditions near sea level, makes fascinating reading (Wilkes, 1845; reprinted by Barnard, 1990), as does the description of the rather elaborate scientific observation camp set up at "Pendulum Peak" on the rim of Moku'āweoweo, the first geophysical observatory in the Hawaiian Islands (fig. 36).

The missionary doctor Gerrit P. Judd (fig. 37) had helped outfit the Wilkes expedition. He later made a harrowing escape from the rising lava in Halema'uma'u lava lake (fig. 38). This passage is quoted from his own memoirs:

> Let down by the hands of a native, I had descended six or eight feet of the basin of a cooled caldron 28 feet deep and 200 wide, and crept along under a ledge where I was crouched down on my feet collecting *Pele's hair,* when the fall of a few stones warned me that an eruption was about to take place, and the next instant the bottom opened 50 feet from me like an immense bubble eight or ten feet in diameter and with a tremendous noise projected a column of lava to a height far above the bank or margin of the caldron. The color of this jet was of the most perfect

crimson and the heat and glaring too great for the eye to look on. I raised myself to an erect posture, turned my face to the wall with my hands upon a projecting ledge above me, which I found it impossible to mount without assistance, nor could I resume my former position and retrace the way I came on account of the intense heat....

When I had given up all and resigned myself into His hand, Kalama appeared on the bank, put out his hands, and seized one of mine, which enabled me by an extraordinary effort to throw myself out. (Judd, 1911, p. 129)

A few years before Wilkes' visit, the Reverend Titus Coan (fig. 39) had arrived to take over the Hilo mission, which he was to serve for over 40 years. Coan was an avid and astute observer of volcanic activity. He and Dana became friends, and they initiated what became a lifelong correspondence concerning the activity of Kīlauea and Mauna Loa. Coan visited the area of the 1840 eruption and recorded what he observed in an account even more detailed than the reports of the Wilkes expedition. Coan also witnessed many eruptions of Mauna Loa between 1843 and 1881 and made frequent trips to view Kīlauea's activity at its summit. By 1851 he was sending letters on the volcano to Dana, who published them in *Silliman's Journal* (later, *the American Journal of Science*).

W. D. Alexander, the earliest surveyor in the Hawaiian Islands, warmly acknowledged Coan's abilities as an observer:

Although he had not enjoyed any special scientific training, and made no pretensions to the character of a professional geologist, he was a good observer and of sound judgement.... To him Geology is indebted for a continuous record of the Hawaiian volcanoes for more than forty years.... No history of the two volcanoes of Mauna Loa and Kīlauea can be written which will not be largely based on Mr. Coan's writings. (L. B. Coan, 1884, p. 218)

It is interesting that in his dialogues with Dana, Coan's ideas have proved to be correct on every issue on which they disagreed. Dana's formal training as a scientist, with which he could provide a theoretical basis for how volcanoes *should* work, was no match for Coan's powers of pure observation and his ability to infer volcanic mechanisms from his own observations. For example, Dana was convinced that lava flows could not travel great distances from their vents. He reasoned, therefore, that long lava flows required fissure systems as long as the flow itself. Coan was able to observe the formation of lava tubes (see fig. 126 and accompanying caption) and during his lifetime tried in vain to convince Dana that flows could travel long distances in tubes of their own making, requiring no separate source beneath the flow. Some years after Coan died, Dana came around to Coan's way of thinking and published a retraction:

The many openings through the crust of a stream into the tunnels, which give out vapors and often have the shape of jagged cones, suggest the possibility that a fissure may exist beneath in these and similar places for the discharge of lava and vapors. But the idea that such fissures generally underlie a lava-stream (which I formerly thought probable) is opposed by Mr. Coan; and there are not facts to sustain it. (Dana, 1891, p. 239)

Even so, Dana failed to understand fully the implications of Coan's work; his discussion continued with a series of questions regarding the 1881 lava flow near Hilo:

The small capacity of the tunnel entered near Hilo suggested the following queries: How much of the lava of a stream a mile wide runs in tunnels? Does the little width of the tunnel, and thereby of the supply stream, account for the difference of velocity in the tunnels and at the front? If so, the exit should be as free as that from a faucet, or the arrangements would not work. How many such tunnels exist side by side? Does a single tunnel continue on for twenty or thirty miles as an uninterrupted lava-duct? We should infer that for a large stream the system of tunnels would become a very complicated one.

Dana did not have the benefit of near-continuous observation of the 1855–1856 lava flow that had also moved toward Hilo, and Coan, who did, had answered all of those questions in articles sent to Dana's own journal (Coan, 1856)!

Much later Thomas A. Jaggar, founder of the Hawaiian Volcano Observatory, acknowledged Coan as follows: "Coan without apparatus or endowment was an institution, a first Hawaiian Volcano Observatory, and in actual output he was a better observer and recorder than some institutions which have been elaborately equipped" (Jaggar, 1913, p. 3).

Another Hilo missionary family, the David Lymans (fig. 40), were good friends of the Coans and also contributed significantly to our understanding of early volcanic and seismic activity. In 1833 Sarah Joiner Lyman began a diary in which she recorded every earthquake felt in Hilo (fig. 41). This diary was continued by the family through the early part of the twentieth century, overlapping the time when Hawaiian Volcano Observatory began keeping systematic observations (Wyss et al., 1992). Sarah Lyman's observations were sufficiently detailed that they have been used by Robert Koyanagi, former observatory staff seismologist, to estimate locations, and even magnitudes, of the larger nineteenth-century earthquakes—a significant contribution to our ability to estimate seismic hazard in Hawai'i (Wyss and Koyanagi, 1992).

Chester S. Lyman, an astronomer and physicist (and a relative of the Lymans of Hilo), visited Kīlauea in 1846 and made some important observations on the mechanics of lava movement in the caldera. He was the first to note that the crater floor was being raised by lava coming in from below, as well as by

overflow from above. He made a map (fig. 42), which was published much later by Dana (1887). Lyman was also the first to recognize the insulating properties of basaltic lava by noting the unexpectedly long time it took to burn a Panama hat that had accidentally blown onto the surface of an active flow (Lyman, 1851).

William Brigham (fig. 43), who later became the first director of the Bishop Museum, visited Hawai'i in 1864–1865. The activity in Kīlauea had continued, gradually obliterating the "black ledge" that had been so prominent in earlier times (figs. 17, 44). Brigham made a crude sketch map of Kīlauea summit (fig. 45), showing the location of various prominent, if ephemeral, features. His studies led to publication of the first chronology of eruptions on the island of Hawai'i (Brigham, 1868).

By 1865, interest in Kīlauea was so great that a rest house, where weary travelers could obtain food and lodging, was built at the summit (Olson, 1941; fig. 46). This first Volcano House, constructed of grass thatch similar to that of native Hawaiian dwellings, was situated some distance from the edge of Kīlauea caldera. An improved wooden building was constructed in 1877; this building has survived for over a century and currently houses the Volcano Art Center in Hawaii Volcanoes National Park. The missionary Orramel H. Gulick provided a guest register (fig. 47), in which he tendered the following invitation to travelers: "Travelers and passersby are requested by the donor of this book to record their names in it and to note all, or any, volcanic phenomena that may come under their notice during their stay or at the time of their visit. By so doing, this record may become of great value, some years hence, to the scientific world. [signed] O. H. Gulick, 2 Feb 1865" (Bevens, 1988).

Scientists and lay persons alike responded, and, as Gulick intended, the register became an important source book for later monographs on the history of Kīlauea and Mauna Loa activity. A compilation of particularly noteworthy quotations and drawings from the register has been published (Bevens, 1992).

Mark Twain was one of the better-known early visitors to Kīlauea. His tongue-in-cheek description of lava-lake activity (fig. 48), dated June 7, 1866, in the *Volcano House Register,* reads as follows:

> Visited the crater, intending to stay all night, but the bottle containing the provisions got broke and we were obliged to return. But while we were standing near the South Lake — say 250 yards distant — we saw a lump of dirt about the size of a piece of chalk. I said in a moment, "There is something unusual going to happen." But nothing happened. Not that time. But soon afterwards we observed another clod of about the same size: it hesitated — shook — then let go and fell into the lake.
>
> Oh, God! it was awful!
>
> We then took a drink.
>
> Few visitors will ever achieve the happiness of two such experiences as the above in succession.
>
> While we lay there, a puff of gas [fig. 49] came along, and we jumped up and galloped over the rough lava in the most ridiculous manner, leaving our blankets behind. We did it because it is fashionable, and because it makes one appear to have had a thrilling adventure.
>
> We then took another drink.
>
> After which we returned and camped a little closer to the Lake.
>
> I mused and said: "How the stupendous grandeur of this magnificently terrible and sublime manifestation of celestial power doth fill the poetic soul with grand thoughts and grander images, and how the overpowering solemnity" —
>
> (Here the gin gave out. In the careless hands of Brown the bottle broke.) (*Daily Hawaiian Herald,* Dec. 5, 1866)

The year 1868 was an action-filled one for Hawaiian volcanoes. A Mauna Loa summit eruption on March 27 preceded an earthquake swarm beneath the southern flank of the mountain—with hundreds of felt events—that culminated in a shock on April 2 estimated at magnitude 8, the largest earthquake yet documented in Hawai'i (figs. 7, 50). In response to the earthquake, coastal areas abruptly subsided, producing a tsunami that caused much devastation and loss of life along Hawai'i's southern coast. The earthquake also triggered a mud avalanche that covered a small village. Three closely spaced eruptions followed, one each at Kīlauea's summit and southwest rift zone, and one on Mauna Loa's southwest rift zone. Titus Coan's report of the earthquake, paraphrased by his son, reads as follows:

> . . . at 4 P.M. on the 2d of April, 1868, an event occurred which defies description. Such a convulsion has no parallel in the memory, the history, or the traditions of the Hawaiian Islands. The shock was awful. The crust of the earth rose and sunk like the sea in a storm. The rending of the rocks, the shattering of buildings, the crash of furniture, glass, and earthenware, the falling of walls and chimneys, the swaying of trees, the trembling of shrubs, the fright of men and animals, made throughout the southern half of Hawai'i such scenes of terror as had never been witnessed before. The streams ran mud; the earth was rent in thousands of places; and the very streets in Hilo cracked open, an occurrence as much out of character in Hilo as it would be in New York. . . .
>
> In the district of Ka-u more than three hundred shocks were counted upon this terrible day. . . . By the culminating shock nearly every stone-wall and house in Ka-u was demolished in an instant. (T. M. Coan, 1871, pp. 569–570, superseded by pp. 893–894)

This earthquake is interpreted today as release of strain on Mauna Loa's south flank from pressure of unerupted magma

Figure 29. Lieutenant (later Captain) Charles Wilkes, leader of the U.S. Exploring Expedition of 1838–1841 (U.S. Ex. Ex.) (Viola and Margolis, 1985, p. 188).

Figure 30. James D. Dana, geologist with the U.S. Ex. Ex. Already well known for his *System of Mineralogy*, published in 1837, Dana is considered by some to be America's first volcanologist (Viola and Margolis, 1985, p. 88).

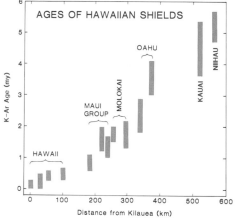

Figure 31. Age and duration of the shield stage of Hawai'i's principal volcanoes. The radiometric ages, determined by the potassium-argon method, become younger, and the time for shield construction becomes shorter, as one travels to the southeast along the Hawaiian chain (modified after Clague and Dalrymple, 1987, p. 20).

Figure 32. Kīlauea caldera daytime view, painting by
Titian Peale, one of the artists of the U.S. Exploring
Expedition (photo courtesy of Bishop Museum).

Figure 33. A nighttime view by the same artist (photo courtesy of Bishop Museum).

Figure 34. Map made by the U.S. Ex. Ex., showing lava flows from the Kīlauea 1840 eruption. Several members of the expedition traversed the east rift zone in both directions, identifying and mapping the various cones and pit craters and the most recent volcanic deposits (Fitzpatrick, 1986, p. 98–99).

Figure 35. The first map of Moku'āweoweo, Mauna Loa's summit caldera, made by the members of the U.S. Ex. Ex. Mauna Loa was not active at the time of the expedition, but the recent appearance of some of the lava in the crater was noted (Fitzpatrick, 1986, p. 92).

Figure 36. Camp on Pendulum Peak, U.S. Ex. Ex., 1841. This sketch by Wilkes appeared in the official narrative of the expedition (Wilkes, 1845). The wall of lava blocks was constructed to protect men and instruments from the harsh conditions at the summit of 13,677–foot–high Mauna Loa (photo courtesy of Hawaii Volcanoes National Park).

Figure 37. Gerrit Parmele Judd. Judd was a missionary doctor who played an important role in the government of the Hawaiian Kingdom. He helped Wilkes obtain a party of Hawaiians to transport equipment to the top of Mauna Loa (Hawaiian Mission Children's Society, 1969, p. 128).

38A.

Figure 38. Halema'uma'u as it might have appeared during G. P. Judd's close escape from a fiery death. **A**, Halema'uma'u by daylight (date unknown), painting by D. H. Hitchcock (Maxon, 1987, p. 106). **B**, Kīlauea by moonlight (1901), painting by E. Bailey (courtesy of Maui Historical Society Museum).

38B.

Figure 39. The Reverend Titus Coan, pastor of Haili Church in Hilo, with his first and second wives. Both Fidelia Church Coan *(left)*, and Lydia Bingham Coan, whom he married after Fidelia's death, occasionally accompanied Coan on his volcano expeditions, and each contributed to the literature on Mauna Loa's eruptions (F. Coan, 1852, and L. Coan, 1881). Lydia assembled a memorial to her husband (L. Coan, 1884) that included testimonials to his scientific acumen, pastoral strength, and gentle nature (Hawaiian Mission Children's Society, 1969, p. 70).

Figure 40. The Lyman family of Hilo: *left to right*, Francis, Emma, Sarah Joiner, David Belden, Rufus, and Ellen. The Lymans were among the most important missionary chroniclers of volcanic and earthquake activity, particularly of events surrounding the great earthquake of 1868 (Hawaiian Mission Children's Society, 1969, p. 142).

Figure 41. Opening page of Sarah Lyman's earthquake diary. The text reads, "A list of earth quakes kept by Mrs. S. J. Lyman at Hilo, Hawaii, commencing June 1833." The original diary is held by the Lyman Museum in Hilo. The entire diary has been published with a commentary (Wyss et al., 1992) (courtesy of Lyman Museum).

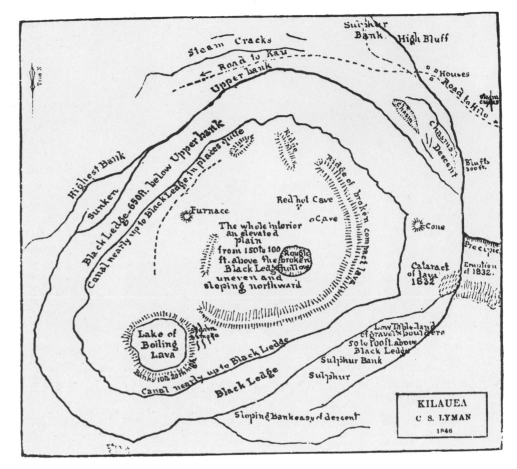

Figure 42. Map of Kīlauea caldera in 1846 by C. S. Lyman, published in Dana, 1887, p. 85; the features shown are described by Lyman, 1851.

Figure 43. William T. Brigham, first director of the Bishop Museum and author of two significant treatises on volcanic activity that were published 40 years apart (Brigham, 1868; 1909) (Paradise of the Pacific, 1926, p. 13).

Figure 44. Kīlauea caldera in 1864, by E. W. Perry. The entire floor is active, and the ledge separating the inner and outer active areas is not nearly as pronounced as it was 20 to 40 years earlier (figs. 17 and 32). (Brigham, 1909, p. 83).

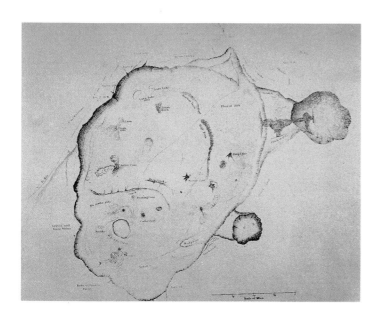

Figure 45. Kīlauea caldera in 1865 by W. T. Brigham. The two lateral craters Kīlauea Iki and Keanakākoʻi are labeled, as are various features on the caldera floor. Lavas of the 1832 eruption on Byron's Ledge (fig. 28) poured into both the caldera and Kīlauea Iki (Brigham, 1868).

46A.

Figure 46. The Volcano House at Kīlauea's summit. **A**, the first building, constructed in 1866, of grass thatch (Brigham, 1909, p. 134). **B**, the second building, built in 1877, with frame of 'ōhi'a wood, exterior walls of imported shingles, doors, and windows. Since 1975 this building has served as the gallery of the Volcano Art Center (photo, circa 1880, courtesy of Hawaiian Mission Children's Society Library). **C**, the parlor of the 1877 Volcano House (photo taken in 1895) (courtesy of the Volcano House).

46B.

46C.

Figure 47. Front page of the *Volcano House Register,* dated February 2, 1865. The original register is held by Hawaii Volcanoes National Park library; it was transcribed by D. Bevens in 1988. Copies of the transcription can be seen at the Hawaii Volcanoes National Park and Hawaiian Volcano Observatory libraries. A selection of the most trenchant observations, comments, poems, and drawings has been published (Bevens, 1992) (USGS photo).

Figure 48. Halemaʻumaʻu Crater in 1868, as it might have looked to Mark Twain on his visit two years earlier (T. M. Coan, 1871, p. 561).

Figure 49. Gas release from Halemaʻumaʻu lava lake in *Um Die Welt*, 3/31/1883 (courtesy of Bishop Museum).

50A.

50C.

Figure 50. The great earthquake of 1868. **A**, "Scene in Waiohinu, Hawaii. The foreground shows how the walls [of the Waiʻōhinu Church] were thrown down; and the hill in the distance is the one from which thousands of tons of earth were thrown in a solid mass by the force of the earthquake, April 2d, 1868" (postcard photograph and comment by H. L. Chase, courtesy of Bishop Museum). **B**, "Mud flow in Kau, Hawaii, caused by the Earthquake of April 2, 1868. The earth shot from the hill a distance of three miles in three or four minutes' time, the flow being from 5 to 30 feet (2 to 9 meters) in depth, destroying houses, burying alive 31 people, and over 1000 head of cattle, horses, and flocks of goats" (postcard photograph and comment by H. L. Chase, courtesy of Bishop Museum). **C**, fanciful depiction of the great Wood Valley landslide of 1868 (T. M. Coan, 1871, p. 570). **D**, "Honuapo, in the District of Kau, Hawaii, where the Tidal Wave caused by the earthquake of April 2, 1868, swept the Catholic Church and a large village into the sea, destroying the lives of a number of people" (postcard photograph and comment by H. L. Chase, courtesy of Bishop Museum). **E**, "Place in Kahuku, Hawaii, where the Eruption of April 7th, 1868, confined five people between two streams of burning lava for a week before they could be rescued from their perilous position" (postcard photograph and comment by H. L. Chase, courtesy of Bishop Museum).

50B.

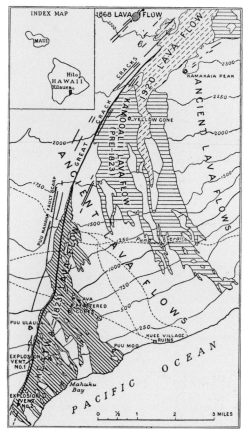

50D.

50E.

Figure 51. Harold Stearns' 1926 map of the lava flows on Kīlauea's southwest rift zone. Note the patch of 1868 lava just below the upper margin of the map, and the 1823 lava extending to the ocean from its source vents on the great crack. Stearns was the first to depict correctly the location of these flows on a map. His placement of the 1868 lava, from field traverses using a topographic map, fits exactly the description given by Titus Coan, 1869, p. 91 (Stearns, 1926, p. 339).

beneath the rift zones, a process analogous to that more recently observed at Kīlauea, where a magnitude 7.2 earthquake struck Kīlauea's south flank on November 29, 1975 (see fig. 27).

Coan's account continues with a quotation from Frederick S. Lyman describing the 1868 earthquake and the accompanying Wood Valley avalanche.

"First the earth swayed to and fro north and south, then east and west, then round and round, up and down, in every imaginable direction, for several minutes; everything crashing about us, the trees thrashing as if torn by a mighty rushing wind. It was impossible to stand; we had to sit on the ground, bracing with hands and feet to keep from rolling over. In the midst of it we saw burst out from the mountain, about a mile and a half to the north of us, what we supposed to be an immense river of molten lava" (it was an avalanche of red earth), "which rushed down its headlong course across the plain below, apparently bursting up from the ground, and throwing rocks high in the air, and swallowing up everything in its way, — trees, houses, cattle, horses, goats, and men. It went three miles in less than three minutes' time." This discharge was so sudden that there was no escape for those within its range. The torrent of earth, shaken by the volcanic convulsion from the flank of the mountain, instantaneously buried a village with its thirty-one inhabitants, and five or six hundred head of cattle. (p. 570, superseded by p. 894)

The intensity of the experience led to exaggerated claims, such as mention of an undersea eruption and a point of land rising out of the sea, neither of which could be confirmed. Coan later commented on these accounts: "Optical delusion and excited imagination often see unreal visions. During the terrific eruption and the rending earthquakes of 1868, men and women of entire veracity saw, as they thought, rivers of fire come down from the mountain and plunge into the sea, within three miles

of them, and all this in open day, with nothing to obstruct their view, and yet, on going to the place where this lava flowed, as they asserted in all honesty, there was no mark or smell of fire" (Coan, 1880, p. 72).

In a report for the *American Journal of Science*, accurately describing the earthquake, tsunami, mudflow, and eruptions, Coan located and described five small patches of lava that appeared on Kīlauea's southwest rift zone (Coan, 1869). Subsequent mapmakers ignored this detail and confused the 1868 Kīlauea lava with lava of the earlier 1823 eruption that had gone to the ocean. It was not until 1926 that Harold Stearns produced an accurate map (fig. 51) showing Coan's patches of lava exactly where he had described them.

Through the latter part of the nineteenth century, Kīlauea continued to fascinate artists (fig. 52). Halemaʻumaʻu was depicted by many persons, among them Lady Constance Gordon-Cumming, one of the first non-native women to visit Kīlauea. Another woman, Isabella Bird (fig. 53), traveled entirely around the island on horseback, visiting the summits of both Kīlauea and Mauna Loa. She and businessman-turned-amateur-scientist William Lothian Green camped on the edge of Mokuʻāweoweo in 1873, viewing the only continuous summit activity at Mauna Loa in historical time (fig. 54). She later published her adventures in a lively book entitled *Six Months among the Palm Groves, Coral Reefs, and Volcanoes of the Sandwich Islands* (Bird, 1875).

The first scientific studies of the products of Hawaiian eruptions were made in the 1870s. One such study was an examination of Pele's hair, the spun glass fibers commonly associated with lava fountains that fascinated all of the early observers (fig. 55). The structure of Pele's hair was depicted in an early camera lucida drawing, using for the first time in Hawaiʻi the revolutionary technique, then only 25 years old, of examining finely crushed or thinly sliced rocks through a microscope.

The Mauna Loa eruption of 1880–1881 was another important event in the history of Hawai'i's volcanoes. Lava from the eruption, which lasted for nearly a year, came close enough to threaten the then-small town of Hilo. Titus Coan published descriptions of the flowing lava and the threat to Hilo (this was the last eruption he saw before his death). Furneaux painted his view of the flow in the early stages of the eruption as it appeared from Hilo (fig. 56). For comparison, Figure 57 shows the 1984 eruption of Mauna Loa from a similar vantage point; this time, lava came to within a few kilometers of the more densely populated town of today. Two other paintings by Furneaux depict the house of John Hall, upslope from Hilo, before the 1881 eruption, and afterward (fig. 58).

More mapping of volcanoes was completed in the 1880s. By that time the Hawaiian Government Survey was charged with making detailed maps of the summit calderas of both Kīlauea and Mauna Loa (fig. 59).

In 1880 Captain Clarence Dutton (fig. 60) became the U.S. Geological Survey's first volcanologist after being detailed to the USGS from the U.S. Army Ordnance Corps. One of Dutton's first assignments was to visit active volcanoes in Hawai'i, which he did in 1882. Dutton was the first scientist to view the volcanoes from the perspective of a field geologist. Although Dutton was in Hawai'i for only a few months, his insights into the volcanic processes involved in building the island were profound. His observations of Kīlauea's lava lake and his interpretation of the geology of Kīlauea and Mauna Loa were published in the *Fourth Annual Report of the USGS* (Dutton, 1884).

Five years after Dutton's visit, Mauna Loa erupted again on its southwest rift zone, above vents active in 1868. By that time a government road had been built to connect the eastern and western parts of the island. The road was promptly covered by the lava flow (fig. 61).

In 1894 Kīlauea's summit lava lake, Halema'uma'u, had reached its highest recorded level — about 100 feet (31 meters) higher than the present surface of Kīlauea caldera below the Volcano House. A view of the lava lake at this time (fig. 62) was painted by the renowned artist D. Howard Hitchcock (fig. 63), who later became famous for his depictions of volcanic activity in Hawai'i.

Mauna Loa erupted again in 1896 (fig. 54). The lava in Moku'āweoweo from this eruption was mapped by F. S. Dodge (fig. 64), using as a base J. M. Alexander's map of 1885 (fig. 59A).

Halema'uma'u, following a collapse in 1894, was only intermittently active until 1907, when it again came into continuous eruption. With improved methods of transportation, more visitors arrived to stay at the Volcano House, which provided guides to accompany tourists to view the active lava (figs. 65, 66).

Early studies in Hawai'i contributed significantly to a general understanding of how volcanoes work. Table 2 in the Appendix lists all recorded observations of eruptions through the founding of the Hawaiian Volcano Observatory. Clearly, in the nineteenth century firsthand observations and written interpretations were made mostly by missionaries and by laypersons with little scientific background; scientists later took the responsibility of summarizing these observations for publication in books or monographs. Probably more was learned in the nineteenth century from direct observation of volcanic activity in Hawai'i than anywhere else in the world. Because of Hawai'i's isolation, that information was not widely disseminated, and therefore not completely assimilated into contemporaneous volcanological literature, despite the publication of articles in the *American Journal of Science* and, by 1909, of three books and a USGS monograph that summarized what was known about Hawaiian eruptions.

Figure 52. Late nineteenth-century artists' views of Halemaʻumaʻu lava lake. **A**, "Kīlauea at Night," by Jules Tavernier in 1887 (courtesy of D. W. Carlsmith). **B**, temporary chimneys and fire fountains of Kīlauea by Lady Constance Gordon-Cumming in 1879 (from Gordon-Cumming, 1883, vol. 2, plate facing p. 113).

52A.

52B.

Figure 53. Isabella Bird, the first Western woman to climb Mauna Loa (Barr, 1970, plate following p. 59).

Figure 54. Moku`āweoweo Crater during the 1896 eruption of Mauna Loa, painting by D. H. Hitchcock. Isabella Bird and W. L. Green would have seen just such a view during their one-week sojourn on the summit in 1873 (courtesy of Bishop Museum).

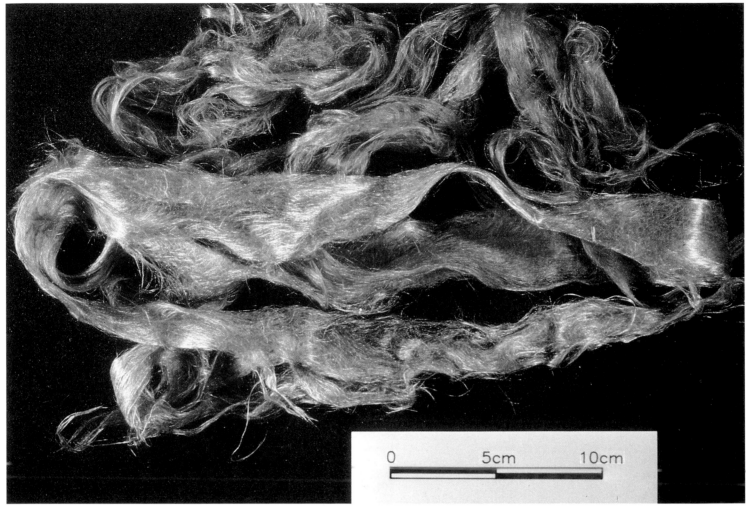

0   5cm   10cm

55A.

Figure 55. Pele's hair, a ubiquitous product of eruptions of Kīlauea and Mauna Loa. **A**, sample collected in 1989 from an active lava tube on Kīlauea's southeast flank. This is the "true" Pele's hair, which has the texture and pliability of human hair; much of what is called Pele's hair consists of coarser, sharper, and more brittle glass needles (USGS photo by J. D. Griggs, 3/89). **B**, "Whirlwind on Hilo Flow," painting by Charles Furneaux, shows Pele's hair flying off the surface of ponded lava near the vents of the 1880–1881 Mauna Loa eruption. This is likely to be a mixture of the coarser and finer varieties (courtesy of Bishop Museum). **C**, glass fibers (Pele's hair) in camera lucida drawings by C. F. Krukenberg (1877, plate 3). These are probably the coarser glass needles, as it would be difficult to see details of the finest hair at the magnification possible with microscopes of the time.

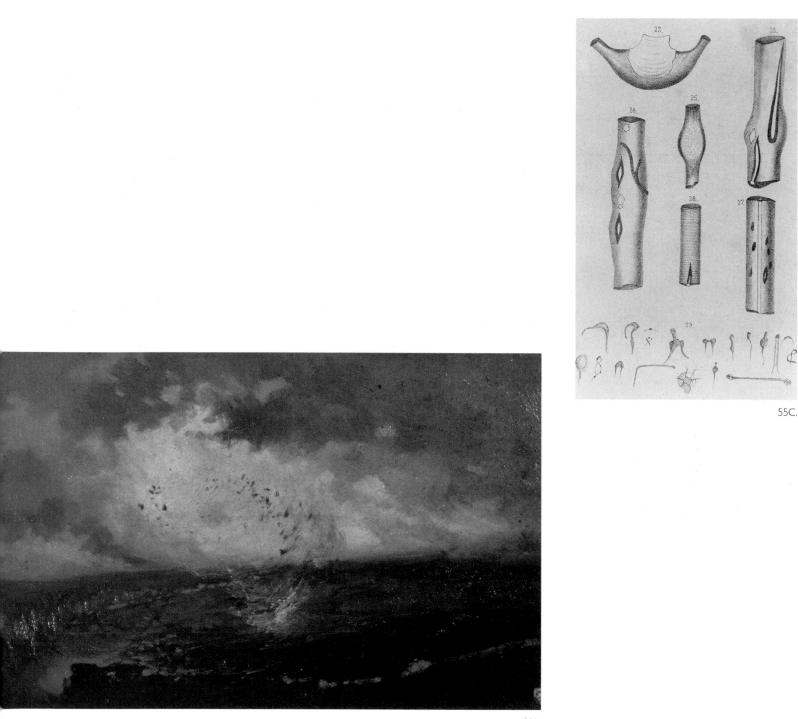

55C.

55B.

Figure 56. A night view of the 1881 eruption of Mauna
Loa from Hilo Bay, painting by Charles Furneaux
(courtesy of Hawaii Volcanoes National Park).

Figure 57. A night view of the 1984 eruption of Mauna
Loa from Hilo Bay (photo 3/84, courtesy of D. Little).

58A.

Figure 58. John Hall's house, located uphill from the village of Hilo, about one mile (1.6 kilometers) from the ocean, paintings by Charles Furneaux. **A**, before, and **B**, after passage of the 1881 flow (courtesy of Bishop Museum).

58B.

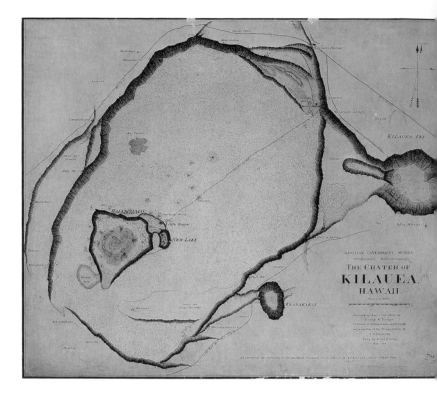

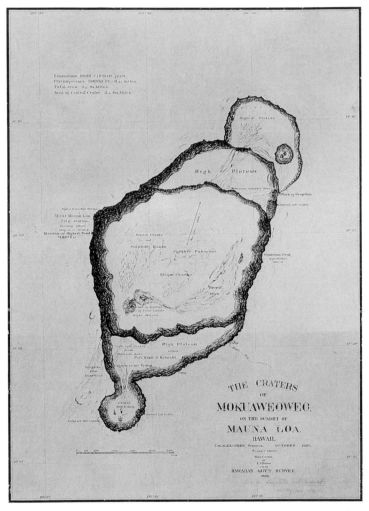

59A.

Figure 59. Early maps of Mauna Loa and Kīlauea made using late nineteenth-century advances in surveying techniques. **A**, Moku'āweoweo as surveyed by J. M. Alexander in 1885 (courtesy of Editions Ltd). **B**, Kīlauea caldera as surveyed by F. S. Dodge in 1886 (Brigham, 1909, p. 163; courtesy of Editions Ltd).

Figure 61. Lava from the 1887 eruption on Mauna Loa's southwest rift zone where it crossed the government road (Logan, 1903, p. 3).

Figure 60. Clarence E. Dutton, U.S. Geological Survey's first volcanologist, whose important monograph on Hawaiian volcanic activity was published following his visit in 1882 (Dutton, 1884) (photo from Rabbit, 1980, p. 33).

Figure 62. Halema'uma'u lava lake in 1894, painting by D. H. Hitchcock. This is the highest elevation that lava has ever reached in Kīlauea caldera. A collapse late in 1894 lowered the lava surface by more than 200 feet (61 meters), and Kīlauea then became only intermittently active until 1907. Eruption was continuous between 1907 and 1924, when another large collapse took place, but subsequent activity has failed to rebuild the crater floor to the 1894 level. Lava from the 1894 Halema'uma'u overflow is still visible, surrounded by younger flows, on the northeast side of the present Halema'uma'u Crater (courtesy of Hawaii Volcanoes National Park).

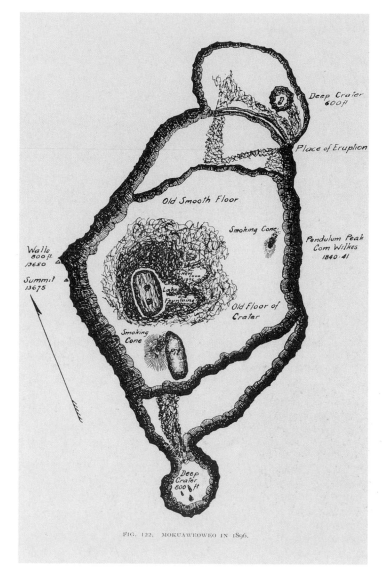

Figure 63. The painter D. Howard Hitchcock. Son of a district judge in Hilo, he attained a worldwide reputation for his landscapes, many of which featured volcanic activity in Hawai'i (Maxon, 1987, p. 77).

Figure 64. Map showing vent locations for the 1896 eruption in Moku'āweoweo, by F. S. Dodge. This was the first map ever made of a Mauna Loa eruption in progress; note that vents are shown for the double fountain depicted by Hitchcock (fig. 54) (Brigham, 1909, p. 195).

Figure 65. Alexander Lancaster, employed by the Volcano House and by HVO. He guided tourists to Kīlauea's active lava lake from 1885 to 1924 (fig. 66) and assisted T. A. Jaggar from 1912 to 1928 (fig. 72) (USGS photo).

Figure 66. A party of tourists at the edge of
Halema'uma'u, circa 1890 (photo courtesy of Bishop
Museum).

AN OBSERVATORY AND A NATIONAL PARK ARE BORN

Around the turn of the century, interest grew in studying Hawai'i's volcanoes in a more systematic fashion. In 1897 the botanist H. B. Guppy, while camping on the summit of Mauna Loa, became convinced of the value of continuous volcano observation. He wrote:

> I hope to be able to study the history of the crater by comparing its condition at the time of my visit with the accounts of its state by previous observers. It is only by such a method of inquiry that one would be able to understand its various puzzling features. By a regular study of this volcano the forecasting of its eruptions would come within the domain of the possible. As we see it now, it displays to us the result of ages of eruptions, each great outbreak leaving some mark behind it often more or less obscured by the work of subsequent eruptions. . . . [fig. 67] (Guppy, 1897, p. 1)

Guppy concludes by saying, "The establishment of an observatory would not be beneath the notice of an enlightened government."

It was 15 years before Guppy's suggestion was acted on.

Another impetus to closer observation of volcanoes was the catastrophic eruption of Mt. Pelée (Martinique, Lesser Antilles) in 1902. Following this eruption, and with the memory of Krakatau's great eruption of 1883 still fresh in their minds, people began to show more awareness of the hazards inherent in volcanic activity. In 1909 Thomas A. Jaggar from the Massachusetts Institute of Technology (M.I.T.), Frank Perret, a renowned American-born volcanologist who made his home in Italy, and Reginald A. Daly, a professor at Harvard University, visited Kīlauea with the idea of establishing a permanent site for volcanological studies. Jaggar and Perret set up the first observing station on the rim of Halema'uma'u in 1911 (fig. 68).

A year later, the Hawaiian Volcano Observatory (HVO) was founded through the efforts of Dr. Jaggar, with support from M.I.T.'s Whitney Fund for geophysical research and from a group of Hawaiian businessmen who formed the Hawaiian Volcano Research Association. Buildings to house the new observatory (fig. 69) were constructed at the edge of Kīlauea caldera at a site presently occupied by the Volcano House. The observatory itself (fig. 70) included Jaggar's office at ground level and the Whitney Laboratory of Seismology in the basement. The early history of the observatory is summarized by Apple, 1987; additional references are indexed in Wright and Takahashi, 1989.

A year before the official dedication of the new observatory in January 1912, Frank Perret had begun studies of Halema'uma'u from his "Technology Station." Perret was fascinated by the constant motion of the active lava lake and had developed an understanding of its circulation system (fig. 71).

To measure the temperature of the lava, Jaggar and Perret employed Seger cones, mixtures of salt and clay, each of which melted at a known temperature. Several cones were attached to a metal pole for insertion in the lava (fig. 72). After removal, identification of cones that were melted and those that were not served to bracket the temperature of the lava.

Lava temperature was also obtained by using a thermocouple. A cable was strung across the 300-meter width of Halema'uma'u Crater (fig. 73A). A thermocouple and a plumber's soldering bucket for collecting samples were lowered via pulley into a perennial central fountain dubbed Old Faithful. Temperature, by current standards, was never measured accurately, but a sample of lava was obtained and triumphantly carried back to the laboratory (fig. 73B).

Another set of experiments involved collection of gases directly from the active lava (fig. 74). Gas samples were obtained in collaboration with E. S. Shepherd and A. L. Day, scientists from the Carnegie Institution's Geophysical Laboratory, who also did the chemical analyses. Analyses of gas collected in 1917 are still some of the best ever obtained from active lava. Shepherd and Day unequivocally proved the presence of water vapor in volcanic gas, a subject of much conjecture in the late nineteenth century.

From 1907 to 1918 the active lava was mostly confined to Halema'uma'u. In 1919 lava from the crater overflowed onto the caldera floor for eight months, fed through a giant lava tube, and was later exposed, to became one of Kīlauea's more spectacular tourist attractions (fig. 75).

The young observatory survived only through the interest of the Hawaiian business community. Lorrin Thurston, who as head of the Hawaiian Volcano Research Association was essential to the establishment of HVO, helped Jaggar with his lava lake experiments. As publisher of the principal Honolulu newspapers, Thurston recorded his experiences at Kīlauea in a series of cartoons (fig. 76). Episode 1 reads:

> On or about January 1917 Proff. T A Jaggar Jr and his able henchman Alex made a successful trip across Halemaumau. The Boat was made of Asbestos re-inforced by armor plate, and had many lavaproof compartments. The Hero is seen standing confidently in the middle of the boat, attired in a fire resisting suit of his own design—with one arm resting lightly on his Lava Pick, while with the other hand he gracefully indicates the passages to his henchman in the rear—

And the sequel:

> On Tuesday Jan 23 several miles of perfectly good pipe was taken down on the lava and amidst great excitement plunged

into the burning pit — (all details were faithfully recorded by L.A.T. so see Advertiser of later date) anyhow it took nearly all day to do the job. During the excitement Demosthenes' [Demosthenes Lycurgus, then manager of the Volcano House] horse was stolen and was seen later struggling manfully under a double burden. (Jaggar, 1945a, plate preceding p. 113)

While work on the lava lake was progressing, interest was growing to have the federal government set aside land to preserve the natural beauty of the active volcanic areas. As early as 1903, W. R. Castle had written in the *Volcano House Register* (Bevens, 1988): "The time has come when the U.S. Govt. might well reserve the whole region from Mokuaweoweo to the sea, at Honolulu [Landing] in Puna, a long narrow strip to include Kīlauea and the line of pit craters to the sea; a comparatively worthless tract of country commercially." Thus was born the idea that 13 years later led to the founding of Hawaii Volcanoes National Park. In the intervening time, local newspapers pushed the idea, two Congressional delegations visited Hawai'i to see the proposed parkland for themselves, and two governors of the Territory of Hawaii lobbied hard for the idea in their annual reports to the secretary of the interior.

Success was finally achieved through the efforts of Lorrin Thurston and Thomas Jaggar, the same two men who had successfully launched the Hawaiian Volcano Observatory. Thurston and Jaggar wrote editorials and accompanied all visiting congressmen on trips through the proposed parklands, including excursions to the active lava lake, extracting from them promises of support for the proposed national park.

On January 20, 1916, Hawaii's delegate to Congress, Prince Jonah Kūhiō Kalaniana'ole, introduced the fourth and final Hawaii National Park Bill, which had been carefully drafted by Jaggar, Secretary of Interior Lane, and Stephen Mather, later

named the first director of the National Park Service. Committee hearings were held, and Jaggar himself went to testify: "There is the same justification for creating a national park about the three great volcanoes of Hawaii that there was for setting aside the wonders of the Yellowstone Geyser district, the Big Trees of California, and the Great Canyon of the Yosemite. The Hawaiian volcanoes are truly a national asset, wholly unique of their kind, the most famous in the world of science, and the most continuously, variously, and harmlessly active volcanoes on earth." Jaggar closed his testimony with an eloquent affirmation of the value of protecting the scientific, as well as the natural, resources: "There is no place on the globe so favorable for systematic study of volcanology and the relations of local earthquakes to volcanoes as in Hawaii, and for this reason alone, if for no other, it would be appropriate to set aside a national park in this wonderland of volcanic activity, where the earth's primitive processes are at work making new land and adding new gases to the atmosphere." (Jaggar, 1916, p. 19)

On August 1, 1916, President Wilson signed the bill into law, thereby creating the twelfth national park. Later in the same month, Congress passed legislation creating a National Park Service to oversee all of the federal parklands. It took another six years for the Park Service to fund the new park. The reasons for the lack of immediate Congressional support were many and complex, epitomized by the comment of a congressman from Oregon: "It should not cost anything to run a volcano" (Albright, 1985, p. 109).

In 1922 Thomas R. Boles was assigned to manage the park. As his first order of business, Boles arranged for the construction of a park headquarters (fig. 77), which boasted a Boles-designed heating system—a nearby steam crack. As Boles reported to his chief, "Being a Department of the Interior structure, it is quite proper that we should obtain heat from the

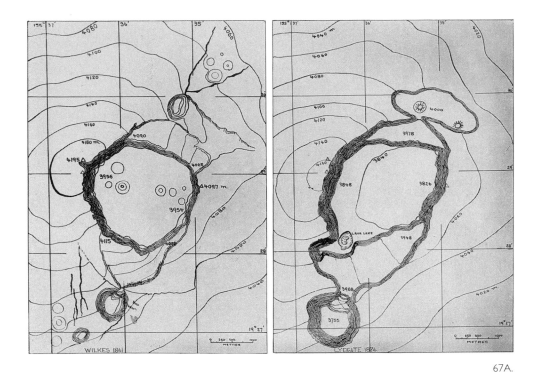

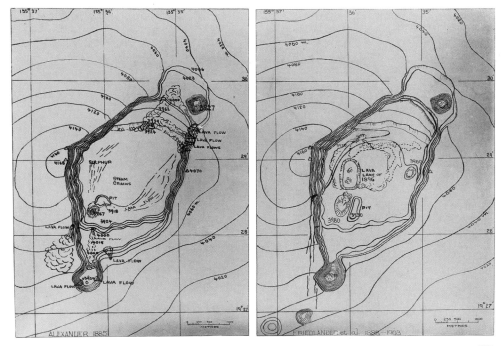

Figure 67. Paired maps of the summit crater of Mauna Loa showing the distribution of lava on the crater floor and eruptive vents at the time of mapping (Jaggar, 1931, p. 3). The lava features depicted were covered by later summit eruptions. Modern computer techniques applied to a Geographic Information System database can now store such information in order to graphically present the history of crater growth. **A**, maps of Moku'āweoweo by Wilkes in 1841 (*left*), and Lydgate in 1874, adapted by T. A. Jaggar to a common scale and contour intervals of 20 meters. **B**, maps of Moku'āweoweo by Alexander in 1885 (*left*), and Friedlaender about 1896, adapted by T. A. Jaggar to a common scale and contour interval of 20 meters. Friedlaender's outline is supplemented with observations by Ridgeway of the 1903 eruption.

67A.

67B.

Figure 68. Halemaʻumaʻu Crater, circa 1910, showing the "Technology Station" set up on the rim of the crater (*right rear*) for Frank Perret's studies of the lava lake. The Technology Station was the predecessor of the Hawaiian Volcano Observatory (photo courtesy of Bishop Museum).

Figure 69. The first Hawaiian Volcano Observatory buildings on the northeast rim of Kīlauea caldera, facing away from the crater (Apple, 1987, p. 1628). The main observatory building is to the left; its cellar housed the Whitney Laboratory of Seismology. To the right is the machine shop and in the right background a cottage for guests of the Volcano House hotel. The unknown photographer climbed a 30-foot (9 meter) drill tower, probably in the late 1920s, to take the picture (photo courtesy of Bishop Museum).

70A.

70B.

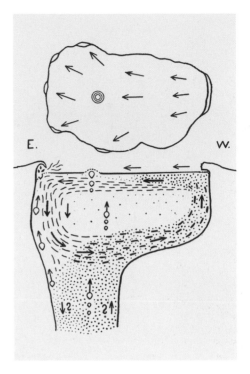

Figure 71. Frank Perret's diagram of the circulation of lava in Halemaʻumaʻu Crater. The upper diagram is a plan view; the circle represents the central fountain "Old Faithful," and the arrows show a west-to-east flow of lava on the lake surface. The lower diagram shows a cross section of convective motion within the lake. Arrows with bubbles depict points where gases are released from the lake to form fountains visible on the surface (Perret, 1913a, p. 345).

Figure 70. Thomas A. Jaggar, founder of the Hawaiian Volcano Observatory, at work (Apple, 1987, p. 1629, 1627). **A**, inside the main building of the observatory. Charts of the seasonal tilt changes at Kīlauea summit, recorded in the Whitney vault, are shown on the wall to the left and above Jaggar (photo courtesy of Bishop Museum). **B**, inside the Whitney Laboratory of Seismology, 1913. Stairs from the main observatory building above come down to the right of the glass partition. Invited spectators stood behind the glass and were not admitted into the instrument room. Jaggar is handling a smoked drum that shows east-west ground movements measured by a long-period Omori seismometer designed to detect teleseisms. Two piers against the far wall hold a two-component Bosch-Omori seismometer. Double springs in the left fore-ground are part of the self-starting Omori "ordinary," a three-component seis-mometer (photo courtesy of Bishop Museum).

Figure 72. T. A. Jaggar preparing to measure the temperature in Halemaʻumaʻu lava lake. A set of Seger cones, fusible mixtures of salt and clay designed to bracket a range of melting temperatures, is shown attached to a metal pole. Seger cones are still used to measure firing temperatures in potters' kilns. Pictured, *left to right,* are Norton Twigg-Smith, Jaggar, Lorrin Thurston (publisher of the *Pacific Commercial Advertiser* and founding member of the Hawaiian Volcano Research Association), Joe Monez, and Alex Lancaster (Apple, 1987, p. 1632) (photo by H. Johnson, 1/11/17, courtesy of Bishop Museum).

73A.

Figure 73. Early lava sampling **A**, clever arrangement of a cable and pulley stretched over the full width of Halema'uma'u, was employed in 1912 to collect samples and measure temperature. Only one temperature measurement was considered "successful" at the time. Even this was low, by more than 100 degrees, when compared with modern measurements on lava under conditions similar to those in Halema'uma'u lava lake. A platinum thermocouple was used, and it is likely that the platinum alloy's composition was changed by reaction with iron in the liquid lava so as to give an erroneous reading (Perret, 1913b, p. 476–477). **B**, Early sampling success, with Perret in the lead. Unfortunately, none of the samples collected at this time made their way into documented collections (Perret, 1913b, p. 481).

73B.

Figure 74. Sampling gases at Halema'uma'u using a specially designed evacuated glass tube attached to a long metal pole. The end of the tube was broken upon contact with the lava, allowing gas to flow in, and the tube was resealed by heat from the lava before the pole was retrieved (Shepherd, 1925, p. 300).

Figure 75. "Postal Cavern," a lava tube that fed the 1919 overflow from Halema'uma'u, southwest of the crater. The overflow lasted seven months and covered the entire northern half of the caldera floor from Halema'uma'u to the area below the Volcano House. A large part of the 1919 lava flow is still exposed against the north caldera wall (photo courtesy of Bishop Museum).

Figure 76. Cartoons poking fun at the work at Halema'uma'u, published in the *Pacific Commercial Advertiser*, 1917 (Jaggar, 1945a, plate preceding p. 113). **A**, taking an excursion in a lava-proof boat. **B**, measuring temperature.

76A.

76B.

Figure 77. The first headquarters of Hawaii Volcanoes
National Park as it appeared shortly after construction
was completed in 1923 (photo courtesy of Hawaii
Volcanoes National Park).

Figure 78. Steam explosions from Halema'uma'u
Crater in 1924. These explosions were triggered by
the withdrawal of magma from Halema'uma'u, allowing water to come in contact with the hot rocks surrounding the conduit. The series of explosions ended
the period of continuous activity at Halema'uma'u
(photo courtesy of Bishop Museum).

Figure 79. Effects of the April 1924 earthquake swarm in Kapoho. **A**, palm trees drowned during subsidence of the coastal section of the Kapoho graben (photo courtesy of Bishop Museum). **B**, railroad tracks twisted by movement on one of the bounding faults of the Kapoho graben (photo courtesy of Bishop Museum).

79A.

79B.

Interior Department of the Earth" (Jackson, 1966, p. 47; parts of the preceding section are quoted or paraphrased from material on pp. 43–46).

Continuous activity at Halemaʻumaʻu ended in a series of violent explosions in May 1924 (fig. 78), caused by groundwater entry into the Kīlauea plumbing system, after withdrawal of magma from Halemaʻumaʻu in February and March. Following the withdrawal but preceding the explosive activity, a series of strong earthquakes shook the Puna district, accompanied by coastal subsidence and by ground movement along faults associated with the eastern end of the rift zone (fig. 79). This was evidence that magma probably drained into the undersea part of the rift zone, a pattern recognized, as mentioned earlier, by J. D. Dana, the early missionaries, and the Hawaiians.

When the explosions ended, Halemaʻumaʻu was left as a greatly enlarged pit 410 meters deep with no lava visible (fig. 80). This brought the early studies of Kīlauea to a close. Through 1934 Kīlauea continued to erupt intermittently from Halemaʻumaʻu; it then became dormant for 18 years.

Beginnings of Instrumental Observation at Kīlauea

Jaggar introduced instrumentation for measuring earthquakes as an integral part of the first Hawaiian Volcano Observatory. The original instruments were bulky (fig. 70B), had low sensitivity, and lacked an easy way to transmit data from sensors in the field to the observatory. Until the mid-1950s, HVO was able to deploy a maximum of only five seismic stations — two at Kīlauea's summit, one on Mauna Loa, and two at outlying stations in Kealakekua and in Hilo. These stations were equipped with field recorders whose smoked paper records had to be changed daily. Independent clocks were used to time the signals coming into the various stations, and the lack of a common time signal greatly reduced the accuracy of the earthquake locations.

Jaggar also pioneered measurement of ground movement associated with eruptive cycles at Kīlauea and at Mauna Loa. A long-period seismometer in the Whitney Laboratory, equipped to measure distant earthquakes, doubled as a tiltmeter, accurately recording the slow tilting of the ground. This seismometer was in use until 1948, and yearly changes of tilt (fig. 70A) were published in *The Volcano Letter* (Fiske et al., 1987).

Baselines for measurement of regional ground movements in Hawaiʻi preceded the founding of HVO. The first topographic survey, made for the Kingdom of Hawaii in 1871, was repeated after Hawaiʻi became a territory in 1897. By 1912 triangulation stations to obtain horizontal changes were established on Kīlauea (Mitchell, 1930). These were reoccupied in 1922 and 1926 (fig. 81), and leveling routes were run to obtain vertical changes (fig. 82) in 1912, 1921, and 1927 (Wilson, 1935). The results showed uplift of Kīlauea's summit between 1912 and 1922 and concomitant deflation between 1922 and 1927, agreeing very well with observations of eruptive activity. The lava lake in Kīlauea caldera had reached a maximum level in 1921, and the entire area visibly subsided in 1924 as lava drained from Halemaʻumaʻu prior to the series of explosions in May.

Attention Turns to Mauna Loa and Hualālai

While Kīlauea rested, Mauna Loa remained active, keeping the staff of the new observatory busy. In 1912 Jaggar had predicted a summit eruption on Mauna Loa before February 1, 1915, to be followed by an eruption on the northeast rift zone within five years (Jaggar, 1912). The first part of Jaggar's prediction was realized when lava broke out in Mokuʻāweoweo on November 25, 1914. Subsequent flank activity occurred on the southwest rift zone, with eruptions in 1916, 1919, and 1926, violating the hypothesis on which Jaggar had based the second part of his prediction, that is, that flank eruptions alternated on the two rift zones. The 1926 eruption destroyed the coastal village of Hoʻōpūloa (fig. 83), the first time in the twentieth century that lava had overcome an established community.

Attention was briefly but dramatically turned away from Kīlauea and Mauna Loa in 1929, when the west coast of Hawaiʻi was struck by a series of strong earthquakes originating beneath Hualālai Volcano. The felt earthquakes continued, and Jaggar issued a prediction (fig. 84), based on the 1868 events, of a large earthquake, tsunami, and an eruption on Hualālai's northwest rift zone, the same rift that had sent lava to the ocean in 1800 and 1801. Fortunately, the earthquake swarm ended without lava reaching the surface, after almost three weeks of frightened anticipation.

Following a brief eruption at the summit of Mauna Loa in December 1933, Jaggar again predicted a northeast rift eruption. In an address to the Hawaiian Volcano Research Association on March 26, 1934, he emphasized the potential danger to Hilo and the responsibility of the association to do something about it (Jaggar, 1936a). He further dramatized the coming eruption and danger to Hilo in a nationwide radio broadcast deliv-

ered on September 11 from the edge of Halemaʻumaʻu during its eruption in 1934 (Jaggar, 1934). This time Jaggar's prediction was correct, and lava broke out on the northeast rift zone in November 1935. As in 1881, the lava turned toward Hilo. Thurston had earlier proposed to disrupt the flow by placing explosives directly into the lava channels. Jaggar implemented Thurston's plan by using aircraft (fig. 85) to emplace the explosive charges. Bombing of lava channels was tried again, under cover of wartime secrecy, on the following Mauna Loa northeast rift eruption in 1942. Both eruptions ended before the effects could be fairly assessed, although Jaggar credited the bombing in 1935 with having stopped the lava flow (Jaggar, 1936b).

Mauna Loa erupted again in 1949, at its summit, followed in 1950 by an eruption on the southwest rift zone that sent three lava flows to the ocean (Finch and Macdonald, 1953; fig. 86). This was one of the largest eruptions of Mauna Loa in historical time. Flows traveled from vent to ocean, 10 km distant, in as little as three hours. A small village, Hoʻokena Mauka, was destroyed by one of the flows.

Figure 80. Halema'uma'u Crater was 1,335 feet (410 meters) deep following the May 1924 explosions and collapse (Bevens et al., 1988, vol. 3, p. 570). Lava returned briefly to the bottom in July 1924, succeeded by intermittent filling from 1925 to 1934, when Kīlauea stopped erupting for 18 years (USGS photo by O. H. Emerson, 1924).

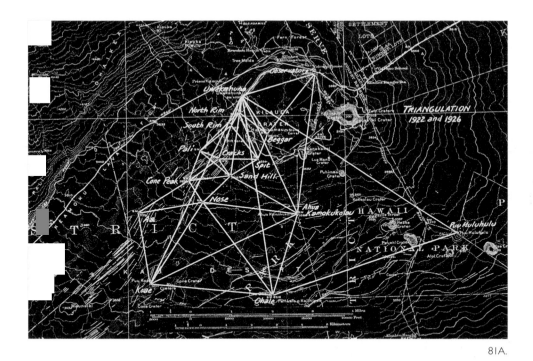

81A.

Figure 81. Results of triangulation at Kīlauea, 1922–1926. **A**, network of triangulation stations (Wilson, 1935, plate following p. 8). **B**, horizontal displacements points to a center of subsidence registered at Halema'uma'u during the great collapse of 1924 (Wilson, 1935, plate following p. 28).

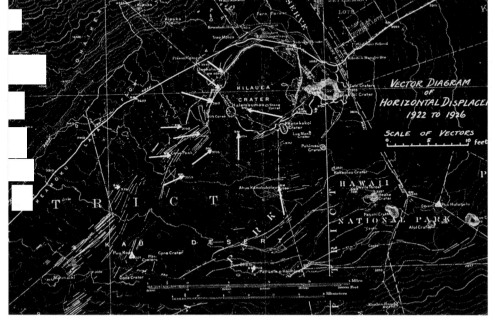

81B.

82A.

Figure 82. Contoured elevation changes at Kīlauea, 1912–1927. **A**, evidence of upward ground movement during 1912–1921. The maximum change is outside the leveling net on the upper part of Kīlauea's southwest rift zone. An eruption occurred on this rift zone in 1919–1920, and the changes probably reflect inflation preceding and following the eruption, as well as intrusion during the eruption (Wilson, 1935, plate following p. 52). **B**, a bull's eye of subsidence defines the great collapse of Halema'uma'u in May 1924. Note how well the vertical changes measured between 1921 and 1927 agree with the center of deflation, measured by triangulation, during the same period (fig. 81B) (Wilson, 1935, plate following p. 54).

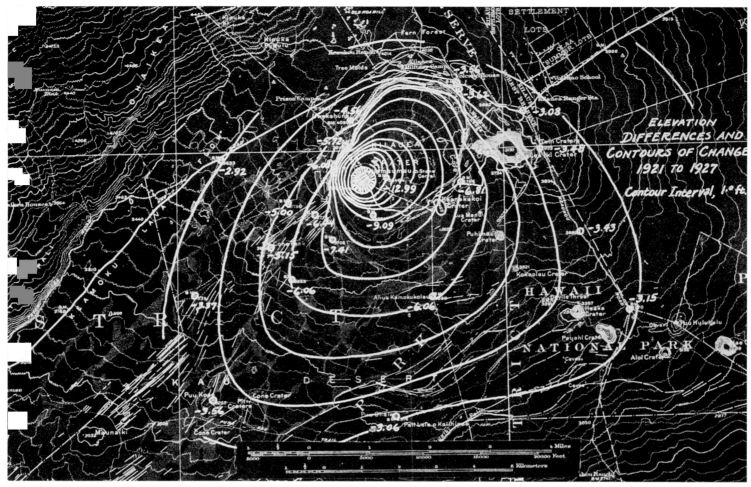

82B.

Figure 83. The destruction of Ho'ōpūloa village on the south Kona coast during the 1926 eruption of Mauna Loa. The 'a'ā flow originated on the southwest rift zone and reached the village in about 48 hours (photo by Tai-Sing Loo, 4/18/26, courtesy of Hawaiian Historical Society Library).

Figure 84. Seismic crisis in West Hawai'i (Jaggar, 1929). Tremors were reported by persons at the Pu'u Wa'awa'a ranch, seven miles north of the summit of Hualālai Volcano, beginning September 19, 1929. The swarm reached maximum intensity during the week of October 2, with up to 200 felt shocks per day, and gradually diminished over the next month. Because of the absence of a seismic network, the earthquakes could not be precisely located, but the distribution of felt reports made it likely that they originated beneath the northwest rift zone of Hualālai, the same rift zone from which the 1800–1801 eruptions had originated (fig. 7) (anonymous, 1929).

ERUPTION OF HUALALAI PREDICTED BY JAGGAR

He Sounds Warning as Hawaii Experiences Severest Earthquake in Series of 150.

Wireless to THE NEW YORK TIMES.
HONOLULU, Hawaii, Sept. 26. —

85A.

85B.

Figure 85. Bombing of the 1935 eruption of Mauna Loa (Jaggar, 1936b, pp. 1, 6). **A**, two-engine plane used on the bombing mission (11th Photo Section, U.S. Army). **B**, explosion from a bomb hitting the lava field. This bomb missed the main channel, shown as a bright line going from lower middle to middle right of the photo (Maehara photo).

Figure 86. The eruption of 1950 sent lava down steep slopes on the west flank of Mauna Loa. Vents from this three-week eruption migrated down the southwest rift zone, sending three flows to the ocean in 3 to 17 hours from the time that lava appeared on the surface, a maximum advance rate of over 3 kilometers per hour. This was the most voluminous Mauna Loa eruption thus far in the twentieth century (Finch and Macdonald, 1953, p. 58).

Figure 87. Halema`uma`u Crater during the eruption
of 1952. This six-month eruption, the first since 1934,
addèd 300 feet (92 meters) of lava to the crater floor
(Macdonald, 1955, plate 6).

VOLCANO WATCHING COMES OF AGE

Jerry Eaton and the Creation of a Modern Observatory

The 1950s represent a major turning point for volcano studies in Hawaiʻi, marked by two events. The first was Kīlauea's return to active status in 1952, defined by a long eruption in Halemaʻumaʻu Crater (fig. 87) that began the present decades-long cycle of activity. The second was the arrival of Jerry Eaton (fig. 88), a young seismologist, who was assigned to the HVO staff in 1953. Over the next eight years, Eaton introduced improved instrumentation for measuring both earthquakes and the ground movements that accompany earthquakes and eruptions. By 1958 Eaton had enlarged the seismic network at Kīlauea to four stations with high sensitivity, all on a common time base, and all directly wired to smoked-drum recorders located at the observatory. For the first time, small earthquakes precursory to eruptions could be systematically detected and located. The bank of recorders (fig. 89) showed, at a glance, the day's earthquake activity.

Eaton also arranged for the construction of a new vault near Uwēkahuna bluff (the site of the observatory since 1948) in which he installed instruments to replace those in the original Whitney Laboratory. Independent stations, also of high sensitivity, were established in Hilo and at Haleakalā on Maui. Subsequently, Eaton added high-magnification seismic stations at Nāʻālehu, Kamuela, and the schoolhouse in Pāhoa. The latter location turned out to be critical in anticipating the 1955 and 1960 eruptions on Kīlauea's lower east rift zone. Tilt recorded at the newly-installed Pāhoa seismometer showed that the rift zone was inflating in early 1955, an important precursory sign of the eruption that began in February of that year. By the time Eaton left, there were 12 stations operating, the beginning of a true seismic network.

Eaton also systemized measurement of ground deformation, introducing a new method to detect subtle changes in the slope of the land surface (tilt), based on the principle of water seeking its own level (fig. 90). The water-tube, or "wet" tilt, method was both sensitive to very small changes in ground tilt and more accurate than the seismometric method, as the change in water level was directly correlated with uplift or subsidence of the ground. One set of three tilt pots was mounted on the walls of the new vault constructed at Uwēkahuna. Other tilt stations were established by building triangular arrays of concrete piers at various points around Kīlauea's summit. For best results, tilt measurements had to be made on overcast nights, which often meant lying in the mud to read the pots. Wet tilting and the laying of heavy cable to connect Eaton's seismic stations to the observatory were a means of initiating new staff members into the modern era of volcano monitoring.

In 1955 Kīlauea erupted on its lower east rift zone for the first time since 1840. This was the first eruption in Hawai'i to be studied using thoroughly modern techniques, with Eaton's instruments in place (Macdonald and Eaton, 1964). The eruption was preceded by four days of intense earthquakes and ground tilting (see fig. 13), causing roads to break before and after lava reached the surface (fig. 91A). The 1955 eruption lasted for four months and seriously affected an area used intensively for agriculture (fig. 91B).

In November–December 1959 an eruption occurred at Kīlauea Iki Crater (fig. 92), followed within a month by dramatic subsidence of Kīlauea summit, during which Halema'uma'u Crater collapsed (fig. 93). The collapse was quickly followed by another coastal east rift eruption in January 1960 (Richter et al., 1970). The 1959–1960 eruption pair is famous in part because of

Kīlauea Iki's spectacularly high fountains and the formation of the first of Kīlauea's passive lava lakes (fig. 94), and in part because of the destruction of the village of Kapoho (fig. 95). The lighthouse on the east point of the island was spared; it can be seen today surrounded by lava that reached the ocean in 1960 (fig. 96). This was the last eruption studied by Eaton before he returned to USGS offices on the mainland. Even as Eaton was taking volcano observation far beyond what Jaggar had been able to do, he was also interpreting data still being gathered using principles inherent in the design of the early instruments. For example, during the 1959 eruption, Eaton interpreted cycles of inflation and deflation of Kīlauea's summit using the long-period seismometer in the Uwēkahuna vault as a tiltmeter, and he was able to track movement of magma into Kīlauea Iki Crater during episodes of high fountaining, alternating with movement of magma from beneath Kīlauea Iki during drain-back into the vent that followed the end of each fountaining episode (Eaton et al., 1987).

The modern era of instrumental observation in Hawai'i begins with Eaton's tenure. Where Jaggar provided the original vision for volcano monitoring, Eaton made many aspects of that vision real, both as an observatory staff member and as Scientist-in-Charge. Over the 30 years following his departure, the network of stations has steadily expanded, and the instrumentation continues to improve; yet the basic philosophy of monitoring and his model of the Kīlauea plumbing system, published by Eaton in a paper entitled *How Volcanoes Grow* (Eaton and Murata, 1960), have not appreciably changed, a testament to the soundness of his approach to volcano monitoring and his insight into volcanic processes.

The complete story of further advances in our understanding of Hawai'i's volcanoes since the 1950s, and of the men and women who contributed to that understanding, would fill another book. In our discussion of these developments, we will emphasize some general and specific ties to the vision or insight of earlier observers.

Thomas A. Jaggar's Vision and Its Realization

The history of the Hawaiian Volcano Observatory and, in a broader perspective, the science of volcanology, owes an enormous debt to Thomas A. Jaggar. In the first *Report of the Hawaiian Volcano Observatory,* published in 1912, Jaggar outlined both the rationale for choosing Kīlauea as a site for permanent volcano observation and the goals of the original observatory (Bevens et al., 1988, vol. 1, p. 7-8):

1. Kīlauea, while displaying great and varied activity, is relatively safe.

2. Kīlauea and Mauna Loa form an isolated center of activity, over 2,000 miles from the nearest active vent, so that the phenomena of these two vents can be recorded without complications occasioned by other nearby centers.

3. Kīlauea is very accessible.

4. The central Pacific position is unique, and is of advantage for recording distant earthquakes through the uninterrupted sea floor. . . . For the study of the deep-sea floor, Hawaii is obviously favorable.

5. [Not included, as it deals with astronomical observation.]

6. There are frequent small earthquakes.

7. The remarkable distribution of both hot and cold underground waters in Hawai'i . . . has an important bearing on agriculture as well as upon science.

8. The territory is American, and these volcanoes are famous in the history of science for their remarkably liquid lavas and nearly continuous activity.

His goals for the early observatory were stated as follows:

1. To erect buildings on the brink of the Volcano of Kīlauea, in which to house the instruments, library, and offices for working up and tabulating the statistics, records and information obtained.

2. To set apart a room for a local museum to exhibit to visitors instruments, plans, diagrams, maps and photographs . . . with a view to securing an endowment.

3. To welcome advanced students from either the Institute [Massachusetts Institute of Technology] or other institutions for special work in the laboratory.

4. To erect subordinate instrument stations, with self-recording instruments, and to employ voluntary observers. . . . It is hoped that eventually some work will be done by the staff of the observatory in the study of tides, soundings, earthquake waves and the movements of the coast line of the island.

5. To send expeditions to other volcanic and earthquake belts for comparative studies.

6. To carry on research . . . in terrestrial gravitation, magnetism and variation of latitude.

7. To make a geological survey of the Island of Hawaii. It is hoped that this will lead to a thorough survey of the whole territory by the United States Geological Survey.

Jaggar concludes by noting that "the main object of the work should be humanitarian — earthquake prediction and methods of protecting life and property on the basis of sound scientific achievement." He also emphasizes the importance of prompt publication of results in bulletins and memoirs.

Jaggar's dedication to making available the results of volcanologic study at Kīlauea to the larger community was realized by publication of the *Weekly* (later *Monthly*) *Bulletins of the Hawaiian Volcano Observatory* between 1912 and 1929. In 1925 he began a new publication, called *The Volcano Letter,* with a broader emphasis, encompassing reports of eruptions around the world, description of new technologies, and reports from other volcano observatories. The final issue, published in 1955, featured a preliminary account of the 1955 Kīlauea eruption. Both series were reprinted, bound, and indexed to make them accessible to students of volcanology (Bevens et al., 1988; Fiske et al., 1987).

"Securing an endowment" for HVO was one of Jaggar's continuing concerns. His Kīlauea observatory began with private funding, but his long-range goal was to have the observatory sponsored by the federal government. In 1919, through his efforts, the observatory was adopted by the United States Weather Bureau, which at that time operated the nation's seismic network. In 1924 HVO was transferred to the United States Geological Survey's newly established Branch of Volcanology. During the Great Depression, funding for the observatory was drastically reduced, and for a time it was managed by Hawaii National Park. In 1948 the observatory was returned to the Geological Survey, which has operated it ever since.

The original HVO buildings were located on the northeast side of the caldera, as was the original park headquarters. In 1927 the Park Service dedicated a new museum and theater (fig. 97), located near Uwēkahuna bluff, the highest point on the rim of Kīlauea caldera. In 1948, when the USGS took over its permanent operation, the observatory traded buildings with the Park Service and moved from the northeast to the northwest edge of the caldera to occupy the Park Service museum. A geochemistry wing was added in 1958. The buildings on Uwēkahuna bluff (fig. 98) served the observatory for several decades, until 1987, when its new and renovated buildings were dedicated on the Uwēkahuna site (fig. 99). The oldest building was returned to service as the Thomas A. Jaggar Museum, now run once again by the National Park Service—a testament to Jaggar's concern that the local citizenry have access to the results of volcanic study. Figure 100 shows the observatory complex in its setting near Uwēkahuna bluff.

Jaggar's humanitarian concerns were directed at minimizing loss of life and property from volcanic eruptions. His motto for the new observatory was *Ne plus haustae aut obrutae urbes* (No more shall the cities be destroyed). As noted above, Jaggar made the first experiments in lava diversion by bombing. Following the end of the 1935 eruption, he published a plan for permanent barriers (fig. 101) to protect Hilo from lava flows originating on Mauna Loa's northeast rift zone (Jaggar, 1937). The barriers were never built, and the concept never tested. Jaggar's plan would have diverted lava to the coast east of Hilo, an area uninhabited at that time. Now the entire coastline is inhabited, and lava diversion would face many legal and logistical problems not foreseen in 1937.

Jaggar's concept of barriers to protect property from lava flows has been applied to protect the multimillion-dollar Mauna Loa Weather Observatory, located at 11,000 feet (3,385 meters) altitude on the north slope of the mountain. A V-shaped barrier (fig. 102) was carefully designed to cause an 'a'ā flow expected from a typical, short-lived northeast rift eruption to pass around the facility. Because of the elevation and isolation of the facility, the diverted flow would not be expected to affect any other developed property. This barrier has not yet been tested by a lava flow.

Hurried attempts were made to protect property from lava during both the 1955 and 1960 eruptions from Kīlauea's lower east rift. Barriers (fig. 103) were hastily erected. They served to divert the first wave of lava, but all were eventually overcome, either from renewed activity at the same vent or from flows from a different direction. These eruptions emphasized the difficulty inherent in protecting property from an eruption lasting more than a few days, especially when diversion efforts were not planned in advance.

Jaggar's vision extended far beyond the limits of Hawaiian Volcano Observatory. He intended the work at Kīlauea to be complemented in a worldwide network of observatories covering many of the world's dangerous volcanoes. In the United States, he was instrumental in setting up an observatory at Lassen Peak following its eruption in 1914, and he made a number of expeditions to the Aleutian Islands to urge that an observatory be established to monitor its frequently active volcanoes. He thus anticipated by decades the idea of permanent, USGS-sponsored observatories to monitor the volcanoes in the Cascade Range and in Alaska, including the Aleutian Chain.

The most far-reaching part of Jaggar's vision, barely hinted at in his rationale for placing an observatory in Hawai'i, was exploration of the sea floor. He first wrote about this in an issue of *The Volcano Letter,* excerpted from an address given to the Hilo Rotary Club on November 11, 1925.

> Hawaii is very wonderfully situated for scientific experiments with the sea-bottom. Could one . . . drain away the ocean, a vast flattish territory would be seen . . . with perhaps some big volcanic domes here and there like Hualalai.
>
> We want to sound by echoes and discover those lost volcanoes. We want to bore into that great plain and get cores of the rock. Is there oil, iron, copper, sulphur, manganese, radium or selenium . . . there? No man knows. . . . If we lay a delicate magnetic instrument on the bottom, electrically connected with Hilo by cable, and thoroughly sealed, is the magnetism extraordinary? If we swing a gravity pendulum in a closed case on the bottom, is the rock enormously heavy? . . . If with our cable attachments we operate a very delicate seismograph in a vacuum on that bottom land, so that the slightest tremblings or tilts of that

wonderful country are written as autographs in the Hilo laboratory, day and night all the year round: will not this be exploration to make the north pole look tame? (Jaggar, 1925)

Twenty years later, following the first successful attempts to map the sea floor and dredge rock samples, Jaggar expanded his vision in a pamphlet entitled *The Vision of Deep Sea Science* (Jaggar, 1945b).

Sea-Bottom Laboratories

With modern floating fibres, cables for anchoring in 2,000 fathoms can be made. With modern electric motors we can bore at that depth. With modern navigation we can anchor a laboratory in mid-ocean, and pull up cores from the rock under the mud and move to other places. . . . Why not a permanent movable observatory of the sea bottom?

Reason for Exploring

Is the bottom of the Atlantic African, South American — or Hawaiian? No man knows. . . Is it volcanic or continental, lava or granite, old or young? Is hot lava oozing forth? . . . Is the volcanic gas making life there? . . . Are there metal ores or precious fertilizers or strange bacteria or metallic lavas? Are there electrical currents, or unusual earthquakes, or cracks, or lava flows, or hot springs, and sulphur beds? No one knows, no one knows, no one knows.

Hawaii Suitable Center

Hawaii is a suitable center for this effort. The University of Hawaii stands ready to found this laboratory.

There have been no modern discoveries on the ocean floor, many made as recently as the 1970s and 1980s, that were not anticipated by Jaggar. These include the deployment of a floating drill rig and laboratory by the Deep Sea Drilling Project, deployment of ocean-bottom seismometers, the discovery, using deep-sea submersibles, of "black smokers" (undersea hydrothermal vents emitting sulphur gases and supporting a unique fauna, including sulphur-eating bacteria, adapted to high temperature and water pressure), the discovery of Lōʻihi seamount, Hawaiʻi's newest volcano, and Māhukona, an extinct and now submerged volcano off the west coast of Hawaiʻi, and the modern mapping of the sea floor using GLORIA and SEA BEAM bathymetry. Still in the planning stages are Jaggar's undersea observatories, now being readied for testing at Lōʻihi seamount and places on the mid-ocean ridges.

Jaggar retired from the Park Service in 1941, and from then until 1947 had an office at the University of Hawaii in Honolulu. Within a decade of Jaggar's death in 1953, the university founded the Hawaii Institute of Geophysics, a large part of whose work has been devoted to oceanographic studies, fulfilling the final part of his vision of oceanographic study in Hawaiʻi.

Geologic Mapping: The Contributions of Harold T. Stearns

Jaggar's seventh and last goal for the new volcano observatory was a geological survey of the island of Hawaiʻi. In formulating this important goal, he oddly ignored Guppy's insightful suggestion (of the 1890s) and did not arrange to map individual lava flows from the many eruptions that occurred during his directorship of the observatory. At best, a few sketch maps were made, often by amateur observers, supplemented by incomplete written accounts of which vents were active, and when.

Geological studies on the island of Hawaiʻi were begun in 1882 by C. E. Dutton, who, however, did not make any maps. In the 1920s Harold T. Stearns arrived in Hawaiʻi to work with the Territory of Hawaii's Division of Hydrography and assumed the responsibility of mapping the geology and evaluating the ground water resources on all of the Hawaiian Islands. About 1940 he was joined by Gordon Macdonald, who provided detailed petrographic information on the various rock formations. By 1947 all islands except Kauaʻi had been mapped and the results published as bulletins of the Division of Hydrography. In the last bulletin in the series, which appeared in 1960, just after Hawaiʻi became the fiftieth state, Macdonald published his work on the geology and ground water of Kauaʻi.

Stearns began his mapping of Hawaiʻi Island in the Kaʻū district and in 1930 published a geological map of the southern half of Kīlauea and Mauna Loa (Stearns and Clark, 1930), the first time that all young lava flows were correctly shown on a map (fig. 51). Stearns and Clark also clarified many older conjectures about geologic processes, such as the nature of various fault systems and the origin of ash deposits. Fifteen years later, Stearns and Macdonald collaborated on a geologic map of the entire island (fig. 104A; Stearns and Macdonald, 1946). This map stood for over 40 years, until the 1980s, when the island was remapped in much greater detail by a team of government and university scientists (fig. 104B; Wolfe and Morris, in prep.) using modern aerial photographs and radiocarbon dating methods for lava flows as old as about 30,000 years (see Lockwood and Lipman, 1980). The new map provides the first summary data on rates of lava coverage for Kīlauea and Mauna Loa, data critical to accurate assessment of volcanic hazard on the island.

Stearns was not directly affiliated with HVO but contributed many insights into volcanological processes, including explanations for the origin of accretionary lava balls commonly formed on top of ʻaʻā flows (fig. 105; Stearns, 1926), an explanation for the explosive interaction of water and hot rock during the 1924 collapse of Halemaʻumaʻu (Stearns, 1925), and the first suggestion that submarine landslides might be important in explaining the concavity of part of the south coast of Hawaiʻi (fig. 4; Stearns, 1926).

Figure 88. Jerry Eaton, on the staff from 1952 to 1961, was truly the second "founder" of the Hawaiian Volcano Observatory. He and a small, dedicated staff developed modern seismic capability on Kīlauea. Eaton designed many of the instruments himself and supervised their fabrication at the observatory. He and his staff also developed a precise, water-based tilt system that quantitatively tracked the inflation-deflation cycles at Kīlauea's summit. His model of the Kīlauea plumbing system has gone unchallenged to this day (Eaton and Murata, 1960) (USGS photo).

Figure 89. Seismic monitoring at HVO, 1967. A bank of six smoked-drum recorders in the main observatory building (fig. 98) was placed behind a picture window overlooking Kīlauea caldera. Visitors viewed these from outside—and HVO scientists from inside—the window, both obtaining an immediate impression of the day's earthquake activity. Each day, fresh glassine paper was smoked with the flame from a kerosene lamp. The previous day's records were removed and preserved with a shellac-alcohol solution. When HVO moved into new quarters in 1986, the smoked-drum method was abandoned due to the fire hazard presented by the smoking room and the increasing difficulty of obtaining recording paper (USGS photo by R. S. Fiske, 9/67).

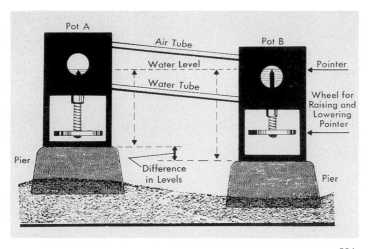

90A.

90B.

Figure 90. Measurement of ground tilt by the "wet-tilt" method. **A**, diagram of the water-tube tiltmeter. It consists of three brass pots connected by water and air hoses, the latter to equalize the pressure on the water surface in each pot. The water level in each pot is carefully read, using a micrometer scale attached to a stainless steel nipple that is moved up or down to the point where it touches the meniscus at the surface of the water (Herbert and Bardossi, 1968, p. 106). **B**, HVO scientist reading the tilt at Kīlauea's summit. In order to minimize fluctuation of the water level due to temperature changes, tilt was usually read on heavily overcast nights (USGS photo by R. S. Fiske, 1/68).

91A.

91B.

Figure 91. 1955 eruption on Kīlauea's lower east rift zone. **A**, earthquakes preceding and accompanying the eruption cracked the road, and a small cinder cone formed over a fissure that erupted through the coastal highway (USGS photo by J. P. Eaton, 7/21/55). **B**, lava (*left*) flows into a papaya orchard (USGS photo by J. P. Eaton, 3/4/55).

Figure 92. The 1959 eruption of Kīlauea Iki Crater.
Fountains from this eruption reached 1,900 feet (585
meters) above the vent, the highest ever recorded in
Hawai'i (photo, 11/59, courtesy of Hawaii Volcanoes
National Park).

Figure 93. Dust cloud generated during the collapse of
Halema`uma`u's floor in January 1960 (USGS photo by
W. Ault, 1/7/60).

Figure 94. The formation of Kīlauea Iki lava lake in 1959. The vent is on the wall of the pit crater, and the rising lake surface reflects the light from the fountain. This is a "passive" lava lake, formed by filling of a pit crater (see Peck et al., 1979). "Active" lava lakes, like that of Halema'uma'u in the nineteenth century, never develop a permanent crust, as they overlie vents that continue to feed lava into the lake. Passive lava lakes develop a permanent crust and cool to ambient temperature once the eruption is over (USGS photo by J. P. Eaton, 12/5/59).

Figure 96. Lighthouse at Cape Kumukahi, spared during the 1960 eruption; lava passed to either side on its way to the ocean. Macdonald (1962) credited the saving of the lighthouse to construction of a barrier close to the vents that effectively slowed down the flow (fig. 103A); the fence surrounding the lighthouse then served as another barrier and divided the flow (USGS photo, 2/11/60).

Figure 95. Kapoho village, with the 1960 lava fountains in the background. The village was overrun about two weeks after this photo was taken (photographer unknown).

Figure 97. National Park Service museum at Uwēkahuna, dedicated April 19, 1927. This building was eventually turned over to the Hawaiian Volcano Observatory (Bevens et al., 1988, vol. 3, p. 957) (photo by Tai-Sing Loo).

Figure 98. HVO buildings before renovation in 1986. The building to the left was the one constructed in 1927 (fig. 97) to house the park naturalists and exhibits; later a connecting ell was added for a theater. In 1948 these two buildings were turned over to the USGS for use by the observatory. The older building was converted into a seismic display room, library, radio room, and offices; the theater was turned into a machine shop. A geochemistry wing (center) was added in 1958; two additional utility buildings completed the facility (USGS photo by D. W. Peterson, 3/11/73).

Figure 99. A new HVO complex was completed in 1986. The building facing Halema'uma'u Crater (*background*) is the original National Park Service museum, renovated as the Thomas A. Jaggar Museum and run, once again, by the National Park Service. The building to the right, the former geochemistry wing, was renovated to provide office and laboratory space for HVO's electronic, shop, and photographic needs. The two utility buildings (fig. 98) were razed to make room for a new building (*left*) to house computer facilities, a library, laboratories for geology, geochemistry, seismology, and nonseismic geophysics, and offices. The tower gives a 360-degree unobstructed view of Kīlauea and Mauna Loa (USGS photo by J. D. Griggs, 3/18/87).

Figure 100. HVO sits on the edge of Kīlauea caldera (*foreground*), with a view to the west of Mauna Loa, whose gentle contour defines the classic shield volcano's shape (USGS photo by J. D. Griggs, 5/22/85).

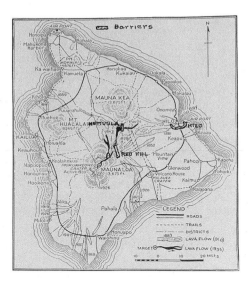

Figure 101. Jaggar's plan for barriers to protect Hilo from lava flows originating on the northeast rift zone of Mauna Loa (Jaggar, 1937, p. 6). These barriers were never built.

Figure 102. Barrier built to protect the Mauna Loa Weather Observatory, run by the National Oceanographic and Atmospheric Administration, from channeled ʻaʻā lava originating on the upper part of Mauna Loa's northeast rift zone (USGS photo by J. P. Lockwood, 11/6/86).

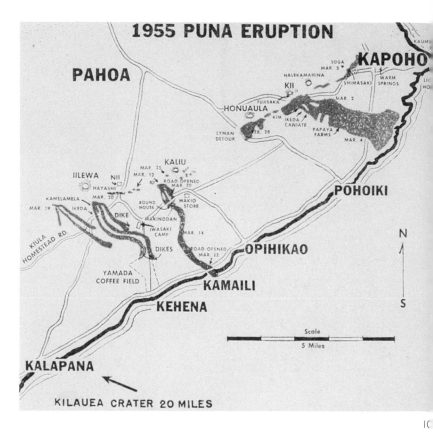

103A.

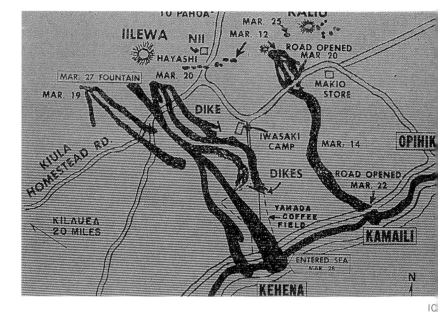

Figure 103. Lava diversion in 1955 and 1960. **A**, bulldozers constructing barriers that helped to slow down the flow heading for the Cape Kumukahi lighthouse in 1960 (fig. 96) (USGS photo, 1/60). **B**, map published in a local newspaper showing location of barriers ("dikes") to protect the Yamada coffee field during the 1955 eruption of Kīlauea (courtesy of *Honolulu Advertiser*, 3/27/55). **C**, map showing Yamada coffee field overrun by breakout from the flow above the dikes. The dikes shown in B stopped the forward movement at that point but were unable to prevent the loss of the coffee field (courtesy of *Honolulu Advertiser*, 3/29/55).

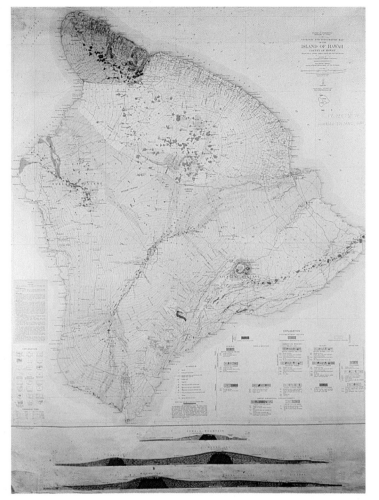

104A.

104B.

Figure 104. Geologic maps of the island of Hawai'i. **A**, the original map, published in 1946. The geology shown is highly generalized. The five volcanoes are distinguished by different color schemes, emphasizing the cinder cones, pit craters, and lava flows of different ages. Historical flows from Kīlauea, Mauna Loa, and Hualālai are shown in darker blue (Stearns and Macdonald, 1946). **B**, revised geologic map, compiled in 1990 but not yet submitted for publication. Flows of historical age are shown in orange. Note the greater detail, particularly of Kīlauea, showing the increased volcanic activity since 1955, and of Mauna Loa, showing how the mapping and dating since 1975 have increased the ability to discriminate older flow units (USGS photo).

105A.

Figure 105. Origin of accretionary lava balls. **A**, lava ball formed on an active ʻaʻa lava flow during episode 4 of the Puʻu ʻŌʻō-Kūpaianaha eruption. Irregular blocks of ʻaʻā clinker become rounded by accretion of molten lava during transport on the flow surface. Stearns (1926, p. 347) illustrated a different process, in which lava balls were formed by repeated exposure to molten lava in a fissure feeding the 1823 eruption (USGS photo by J. D. Griggs, 6/16/83). **B**, field of lava balls on a cooled ʻaʻā surface, Puʻu ʻŌʻō-Kūpaianaha eruption (USGS photo by J. D. Griggs, 5/24/91).

105B.

Figure 106. The central lava pond that developed within Halema`uma`u Crater during the early part of the eruption of Kīlauea in 1967–1968. During that time, the floor of the crater grew higher by overflow from the pond. Later the pond crusted over, but the surface continued to rise as lava entered the lake beneath the solid crust. Both processes, lake overflow and "piston uplift," were observed and documented in the nineteenth century (USGS photo by R. S. Fiske, 4/5/68).

OBSERVATION OF MODERN ERUPTIONS: BUILDING ON NINETEENTH-CENTURY INSIGHTS

After several short eruptions, both at the summit and along the east rift, Kīlauea erupted again in Halemaʻumaʻu Crater from November 1967 through July 1968 (Kinoshita et al., 1969) and quickly developed a lava lake (fig. 106) similar to those active in Kīlauea caldera during the nineteenth century (fig. 62). The lake filled to within 50 meters of the crater rim, but subsequent collapses, associated with flank eruptions, reduced the level of the crater floor. The high lava mark left at the end of the eruption was still visible in the 1990s (fig. 107).

From 1969 to 1974, Kīlauea had a long east rift eruption that built the small satellitic shield Mauna Ulu (fig. 108; Swanson et al., 1979; Tilling et al., 1987). Mauna Ulu lavas now cover much of the route that William Ellis took from Kīlauea's summit to the coast in 1823, including the site of Kealakomo village. The Mauna Ulu eruption was followed a decade later by a similar eruption farther down the rift zone, the Puʻu ʻŌʻō-Kūpaianaha eruption (Wolfe et al., 1987).

Many small cones were constructed during the Mauna Ulu eruption (fig. 109). Some of these assumed the steep shape characteristic of cones that dotted the floor of Kīlauea caldera when the first Western visitors arrived (figs. 17, 52B). A description of this kind of cone building by a member of the Wilkes expedition matches exactly later interpretation by scientists observing the Mauna Ulu eruption.

Each cone was about fifty feet high, and a hundred in circumference at the base; and both in an active state of eruption, — rapidly spitting and disgorging red-hot lava from wide mouths at their summits.... From observations on the spot, and subsequent reflection, I shall hazard an opinion of the probable manner in which these conical craters may have been constructed. The molten mass of lava below increasing in volume, . . . relieves itself by jetting or flowing out, in quantities according to the propelling force, through holes and crevices in the floor of the crater. When flowing out in large torrents, and with much force, it will spread far and wide, as, when in such a large body, sufficient caloric is present to retain it long in a fluid state: but when flowing out in a small stream, or jetting with little force and in small quantities, it soon becomes solid, forming a kind of embankment all round the hole or crevice of exit. Under these circumstances a cone would be rapidly built. In the two cones our party here halted to examine, the lava frequently was not ejected with sufficient force to clear the base. Falling, therefore, on the surface of the cone, and becoming consolidated before it could run down its side, accession of matter was thus received. . . . Beyond a certain elevation, which is perhaps about fifty feet, the lava, under ordinary circumstances, cannot be propelled. Any cone, therefore, having arrived to that certain elevation, would then become quiescent, whilst others of less elevation would increase in activity, or the lava would force an exit through some part of the side of the cone. . . . (Rees, 1841, p. 503)

An aerial view (fig. 110) shows much of the land surface where historic activity has occurred at Kīlauea summit and the upper east rift. Both recent long-lived eruptions, Mauna Ulu and the Puʻu ʻŌʻō-Kūpaianaha series, began with episodes of spectacular high fountaining (fig. 111), which shifted to continuous effusion of lava at a lower rate. The first stage of the eruption that began in 1983 was marked by 47 episodes, most lasting less than a day and occurring at intervals of three to four weeks. High fountains fed mainly ʻaʻā flows (fig. 112) and built the 800-foot high cinder cone Puʻu ʻŌʻō. In July 1986 the eruption shifted downrift and began continuous activity, building a small shield, later named Kūpaianaha. The continuous stage was marked by

the presence of a central lava lake perched over the vent (fig. 113), much like Halemaʻumaʻu in the nineteenth century (fig. 62) and Mauna Ulu a decade earlier. An oblique aerial view of the lava field in 1987 (fig. 114) shows the impact of lava flows on the Royal Gardens subdivision, which was very close to the rift zone.

An interesting aspect of the active lava lakes has been the movement of the cooled surface crust over the still-molten lava below (fig. 115). One of the most commonly observed phenomena is foundering of the crust due to the pressure and release of rising gas (fig. 116). The following passage describing the phenomenon was written in the 1880s by the Reverend E. P. Baker:

> . . . a *lake* of lava . . . will crust over indeed, but then, the crust thus formed, will not for any length of time remain undisturbed; the uprising through the fiery liquid beneath, of superheated steam or gas, tending to uplift the crust above it; until at length, the tension, occasioned by the antagonism to each other of the elasticity of the superheated steam or gas confined beneath, and the downward pressure of the rocky crust resting its full weight on the unwilling prisoner below, becoming too severe to be endured any longer, the crust gives way (the confined gases below of course cannot give way); which giving way is seen to take place somewhat as follows; A fragment of the crust, which has already cracked off from the main body is observed to tilt up and plunge into the fiery sea beneath (cooled lava having a greater specific gravity than molten lava.) Then the next adjoining fragment, unsupported as it is on one side, follows suit, and then another, another and still another; the process coming to an end, only when all the old crust has gone down and been remelted, and a new and thin crust has been formed to take the place of the old; this new and thin crust, after awhile becoming old and thick, and in its turn, going the way of its predecessor. (Baker, 1885, p. 1)

This superb (if syntactically difficult) account matches precisely more modern interpretations of the crustal-foundering process.

Continuous effusion of lava during the Kūpaianaha stage of the current eruption has provided insights into many important volcanic processes. Through the end of 1989, lava from Kūpaianaha lava lake flowed to the ocean through a complex series of lava tubes, similar to those formed during earlier activity at Mauna Ulu. Occasionally parts of the roofs of lava tubes collapse, allowing spectacular views into the lava river below (fig. 117). Samples from both the lava lake and from skylights in lava tubes associated with the Kūpaianaha vent (fig. 118) are taken as they were in Jaggar's day (fig. 73). A cable with a hammer head on the end is lowered directly into a lava river or into fountaining areas near the edge of a lava lake. The sample adheres to the hammer and is pulled up by hand.

When lava first entered the sea, a unique form of tephra—called *limu* for its resemblance to seaweed (fig. 119) — was collected by Hawaii Volcanoes National Park interpreters. The delicate, transparent sheets of volcanic glass are formed when water enters flowing lava, forming a giant bubble, which bursts into flakes of limu (fig. 120). Occasionally a portion of the sea cliff collapses, and lava emerges from a tube directly into the surf (fig. 121). Lava breaks up from surf action (fig. 122) into black sand, which is then transported by longshore currents to form new beaches (fig. 123). Sometimes lava is thrown back explosively onto the shore, building littoral cones (fig. 124). Under water, lava forms pillows (fig. 125).

Early descriptions and interpretations of the formation of Hawai'i's two common lava types—'a'ā and pāhoehoe—are still relevant to studies made during recent eruptions. Titus Coan, with his remarkable understanding of the importance of lava tubes in the formation of pāhoehoe fields (fig. 126), accurately interpreted features of flowing pāhoehoe that we observe

today. The following passage, taken from Coan's memoirs, completed just before his death, describes the 1881 lava flow from Mauna Loa:

> I may add a word upon the curious process by which this lava flow, like others, has made its way over so great a distance from its source.... As the lava first rushes down the steeper inclinations it flows uncovered; but its surface soon hardens, forming a firm, thick crust like ice on a river, and under this crust the torrent runs highly fluid, and retaining nearly all of its heat. In this pyroduct, if I may so call it, the lava stream may pour down the mountainside for a year or more, flowing unseen, except where openings in the roof of its covered way reveal it.
>
> When the molten river reaches the more level highlands at the base of the mountain, it moves more slowly.... The surface of it soon hardens; the lavas below are sealed within a rigid crust that confines them on every side. Their onward progress is thus checked for hours or days....While the lava is held in check as I have described, the uninitiated visitor will pronounce the flow to have ceased. But it is only accumulating its forces. The lava presses down from the source, until suddenly the hardened crust is ruptured with a crash, the lava moves forward again, and a new joint is added to the covered way. Thus overcoming all obstacles, the fusion is kept under cover, and moves forward or laterally in its own ducts for an indefinite distance. It may flow at white heat in this way for thirty or forty miles and reach the sea at a distance of more than fifty miles from the mountain source.
>
> By virtue of this pressure from behind, and of its own viscidity, the lava may even be propelled *up-hill* for a certain distance, if the outbursting rush of lava be directed upon an upward slope. The lava thus grades its own path as it goes seaward. (Coan, 1882, p. 332)

Coan's explanation would be readily understood by anyone who has watched the last two long-lived eruptions at Kīlauea—

Mauna Ulu and Pu'u 'Ō'ō-Kūpaianaha. The last statement would be particularly meaningful to Kalapana residents who have lost their homes, many of which were destroyed by lava moving from land that was originally at a lower elevation.

Earlier, W. D. Alexander, who observed the 1859 eruption of Mauna Loa, compared the two lava types (fig. 127) and gave a particularly apt description of the formation of 'a'ā. This interpretation, which is consistent with our modern understanding of the process, was echoed by both Jaggar and Macdonald, who, if they were aware of Alexander's observations, did not cite his interpretation.

> The difference between "pahoehoe" or smooth lava, and "aa" or clinkers, seems to be due more to a difference in their mode of cooling than to any other cause. The streams which form the "pahoehoe" are comparatively shallow, in a state of complete fusion, and cool suddenly in a mass [fig. 128]. The "aa" streams on the other hand, are deep, sometimes moving along in a mass 20 feet high, with solid walls [fig. 129];—they are less fluid, being full of solid points, or centers of cooling, as they might be called, and advance very slowly. That is, in cooling, the aa stream *grains* like sugar. At a distance, it looks like an immense mass of half red-hot cinders and slag from a foundry [fig. 130], rolling along over and over itself, impelled by an irresistible power from behind and beneath. That power is the liquid stream [fig. 131], almost concealed by the pile of cinders, which has been formed from itself in cooling. (Alexander, 1859, p. 2)

In 1984 Mauna Loa erupted on its northeast rift zone (fig. 132), the first flank eruption of Mauna Loa to be studied using modern instruments and (thanks to helicopters) nearly continuous, detailed observations in the field (Lockwood et al., 1985). The evolution of the channel in an 'a'ā flow was studied by Lipman and Banks (1987), who found that lava in the channel was undercooled and, as the eruption progressed, crystallized with no change of temperature or eruption rate. This process, analogous to the graining of sugar described above by Alexander, contributed to clogging of the open channel, which then overflowed its banks—a process of natural lava diversion (fig. 133) never before observed in such detail.

This section highlights the contributions of early workers to our current understanding of volcanic processes. Succeeding generations of volcanologists will continue to benefit from increasingly sophisticated instrumentation and data analysis. It is important that we not lose our ability to directly observe and interpret what we *see* — a small homage to those who came before us when human resources were all that were available.

Figure 107. The high lava mark left at the end of the 1967–1968 eruption is visible as a prominent horizontal line separating lighter and darker parts of the Halema'uma'u Crater wall (USGS photo by J. D. Griggs, 5/1/91).

Figure 108. Mauna Ulu, a lava shield on Kīlauea's upper east rift zone, built during the 1969–1974 eruption. The summit crater of Mauna Ulu contained an active lava lake whose frequent overflows were responsible for most of the growth of the shield to its final height of 121 meters above the pre-1969 ground surface. Flows from Mauna Ulu filled two pit craters, ʻĀloʻi and ʻAlae, and partly filled a third, Makaopuhi, all of which lay along the old Chain of Craters Road. Lava from Mauna Ulu flowed into the ocean for many months at a time, overrunning much of the trail that Ellis took from Kīlauea's summit to the coast, including the village of Kealakomo (fig. 140B). About 230 acres (1 km^2) of land were added to the island during this eruption (USGS photo by J. D. Griggs, 6/14/89).

109A.

Figure 109. Conical spatter cones of the Mauna Ulu eruption. In size and method of formation, these cones closely match those illustrated, described, and interpreted by early visitors to Kīlauea caldera (figs. 17, 52B). **A**, a small cone (height approximately 20 feet (6 meters)), built during the early part of the eruption (USGS photo by D. A. Swanson, 5/21/70). **B**, a larger cone (height approximately 50 feet (15 meters)), built late in the eruption (USGS photo by R. T. Holcomb, 2/28/74).

109B.

Figure 110. Aerial view of the summit and upper east rift zone of Kīlauea Volcano. The large, elliptical depression in the foreground is Kīlauea caldera, within which is the central pit crater Halemaʻumaʻu. The Hawaiian Volcano Observatory is seen to the lower left on the rim of the caldera. Kīlauea Iki and Keanakākoʻi craters lie on the far side of the caldera to the left- and right-center, respectively. A cloud covers Byron's Ledge, which separates Kīlauea caldera from Kīlauea Iki. The east rift zone begins at Kīlauea Iki, heads first to the right, then swings back to the left in a large arc. Directions to other features are given as clock hands originating at Halemaʻumaʻu: Mauna Ulu is a small, fuming yellow spot at 12:30. Puʻu ʻŌʻō, trailing a large steam plume to the left, lies at 11:00. In the caldera, the lighter lava to the left of Halemaʻumaʻu is the 1919 overflow. The blacker lava at 10:00–12:00 was erupted in 1974 and covers most of the caldera floor not covered by 1919 lava. The very black lava at the left edge of Halemaʻumaʻu and at 2:00 was produced in 1982, the most recent summit eruption of Kīlauea (USGS photo by J. D. Griggs, 1/10/85).

Figure 111. High lava fountain at Puʻu ʻŌʻō. (USGS
photo by C. C. Heliker, 9/19/84).

Figure 112. Lava fountain at Pu'u 'Ō'ō, June 30, 1984. An 'a'ā flow in the foreground is being fed from a river of lava flowing in a channel cut into the left side of the cone (USGS photo by J. D. Griggs, 6/30/84).

Figure 113. Kūpaianaha lava lake, here veneered with shiny, cooled crust, formed after a vent opened about 3 kilometers downrift from Pu'u 'Ō'ō in July 1986. The Pu'u 'Ō'ō cone, at its maximum height of 255 meters, is seen along the skyline (USGS photo by J. D. Griggs, 1/13/87).

Figure 114. Steam rises from the Kapa'ahu shoreline where pāhoehoe flows from the Kūpaianaha shield (K) entered the ocean, beginning in 1987. Earlier 'a'ā flows from the Pu'u 'Ō'ō cone (P) entered the Royal Gardens subdivision (left-center slope). The eastern boundary of Hawaii Volcanoes National Park extends from Pu'u 'Ō'ō to the left of Royal Gardens (USGS photo by J. D. Griggs, 12/28/87).

115A.

Figure 115. Crustal foundering on Kūpaianaha lava lake. **A**, large plates of cooled crust (*dark*) separated by narrow, lighter areas, where incandescent lava is rising to the surface (USGS photo by J. D. Griggs, 2/2/87). **B**, detail, from lake level, of cooler crust being subducted beneath the hotter lava at the edge of a plate (USGS photo by C. C. Heliker, 1/6/87). **C**, piece of crust tilting before being consumed in the foundering process (USGS photo by C. C. Heliker, 11/19/87).

115B.

116

115C.

116A.

Figure 116. Overturning (foundering) of the crust of the 1965 lava lake in Makaopuhi Crater. (Compare this series of photographs with Baker's description of the process quoted in the text.) **A**, overturning begins near the lake's edge. Cooler crust (*blue*) is being over-ridden by hot, molten lava (*orange*) rising along circular fractures that propagate outward (USGS photo by D. L. Peck, 3/8/65). **B**, the overturn propagates in ever-widening circles. The crust inside the outer molten ring tilts before sliding beneath the freshly formed lava surface (USGS photo by D. L. Peck, 3/8/65). **C**, by the end of the sequence of overturns, nearly three-fourths of the lake surface is renewed (USGS photo by D. L. Peck, 3/8/65).

116B.

116C.

Figure 117. Skylight in a tube that was active during the
Mauna Ulu eruption. Such openings, produced by
local collapse of the tube roof, provide a dramatic
look at rivers of lava flowing in tubes of their own
making (USGS photo by J. Judd, 10/21/70).

118A.

118B.

118C.

Figure 118. Modern lava sampling (cf. fig. 73). **A**, sampling through a skylight in a lava tube during the Puʻu ʻŌʻō-Kūpaianaha eruption using a device designed by F. Trusdell. A sampling cable with a hammer head attached to the end is suspended over the skylight, lowered into the river of lava, and rapidly pulled out when lava adheres to the hammer head (USGS photo by J. D. Griggs, 12/5/90). **B**, sampling from Kūpaianaha lava lake. A similar device is lowered into a fountain at the lake's edge (USGS photo by C. C. Heliker, 6/30/88). **C**, sampling success at Kūpaianaha lava lake (compare fig. 73B) (USGS photo by C. C. Heliker, 10/11/89).

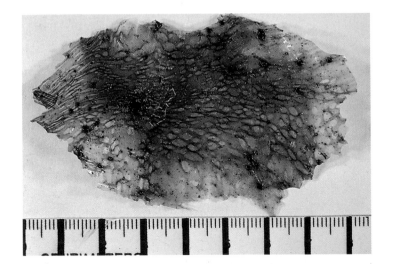

Figure 119. *Limu o Pele* (Pele's seaweed), delicate, translucent sheets of spatter filled with tiny gas bubbles, collected during the Pu'u 'Ō'ō-Kūpaianaha eruption from ocean entries near the former Kūpapau Point (see fig. 138) (USGS photo by J. D. Griggs, 2/25/87).

Figure 120. The formation of limu near Kūpapau Point. **A**, water is trapped within a roofed-over lava stream where it enters the ocean (USGS photo by K. Hon, 12/4/89). **B**, a large, thin-walled bubble, sometimes several meters across, expands and begins to break apart (USGS photo by J. D. Griggs, 10/5/88). **C**, a final explosion sends flakes of *limu* into the air to be deposited on land (USGS photo by J. D. Griggs, 10/5/88).

120A.

120B.

120C.

Figure 121. Collapse of the sea cliff near Kūpapau Point exposes lava streaming from a tube above the surf line. The lava is remarkable for the lack of any temperature gradient across the stream, as evidenced by the uniformity of the yellow incandescence. Apparently the high flow rate and/or a thin shell of superheated gas surrounding the liquid prevents cooling when lava is first exposed to the air (USGS photo by J. D. Griggs, 4/21/88).

Figure 122. Formation of black sand. Lava entering the ocean breaks into large fragments which are quickly reduced to progressively smaller pieces with each wave breaking onshore. Ultimately, the sand-sized material collects near the point where lava entered the ocean and may be transported many kilometers down the coast by longshore currents (USGS photo by J. D. Griggs, 4/13/88).

Figure 123. Black sand at Kamoamoa. **A**, sea cliffs at Kamoamoa campground (see fig. 138) before lava entered the sea during the Puʻu ʻŌʻō-Kūpaianaha eruption (photo courtesy of D. Hamilton, 8/86). **B**, new black sand beach formed a year after lava began entering the ocean 10 kilometers to the east. Now the largest black sand beach in Hawaiʻi, it will probably disappear after the eruption ends. The steep cliffs on which the beach is built are especially susceptible to winter storms that can quickly remove the accumulated sand once the supply ceases (photo courtesy of D. Hamilton, 1/21/88).

123A.

123B.

Figure 124. Littoral cone, about 20 feet (6 meters) high, formed near Kūpapau Point during the Puʻu ʻŌʻō-Kūpaianaha eruption. These cones are formed from material thrown shoreward as lava and water interact explosively. The cone shown here disappeared when the bench of new lava on which the cone was built collapsed in a landslide large enough to be recorded by seismometers many kilometers from the ocean. The largest littoral cones may survive, particularly those built on a stable shoreline during brief eruptions. Littoral cones associated with the eruptions of 1840 (Kīlauea) and 1868 (Mauna Loa) were misinterpreted by Dana, who thought they overlay erupting fissures, and used this notion to bolster his arguments with Coan regarding the viability of lava tubes (USGS photo by J.D. Griggs, 10/5/88).

Figure 125. Pillow lava. **A**, pillows in the process of forming off Kūpapau Point during the Pu'u 'Ō'ō-Kūpaianaha eruption. When lava enters the ocean, its skin is chilled into a spherical shell. As lava continues to enter the molten interior, the shell expands until it cracks, releasing a new pillow, and the process repeats itself as lava moves downslope (photo courtesy of G. Tribble, 10/90). **B**, cooled pillows, off shore from Kealakomo, formed during the Mauna Ulu eruption. The pillows have already acquired a veneer of algae and provide a home for sea life only months after lava entered the ocean (USGS photo by D. W. Peterson, 1/11/74).

125A.

125B.

126A.

Figure 126. Modern observation of lava tubes. **A**, tube transporting lava away from Kūpaianaha lava lake toward the coast (*upper left*). The steaming areas trace the covered path of the tube downslope from the tube entrance at the end of the active lake (USGS photo by G. Ulrich, 2/2/87). **B**, aerial view of the tube delivering lava to the ocean. The neck of the same Kūpaianaha lava pond is now roofed over; the entrance to the tube shows up as a small orange spot in the active pond near the bottom of the photo. A larger plume of steam rises where lava enters the ocean (USGS photo by J. D. Griggs, 4/21/88). **C**, thermal infrared aerial view of traces of two braided tubes delivering lava to the ocean. The tube to the left is the more active and generates a plume of hot water and steam as lava enters the ocean. Titus Coan could not possibly have anticipated so clear a proof of his contention that tubes can transport lava long distances from their source (photo by V. Realmuto, 10/88, courtesy of NASA).

126C.

126B.

Figure 127. Hawaiʻi's two common lava types, ʻaʻā (*top*) and pāhoehoe (*bottom*), from the Puʻu ʻŌʻō-Kūpaianaha eruption. ʻAʻā has a rough surface composed of large blocks of clinker; pāhoehoe has a smooth, shiny, and often ropy surface. These two lava types are recognized worldwide as products of basaltic volcanoes (USGS photo by J. D. Griggs, 2/15/90).

Figure 128. Pāhoehoe sheet flow fed from an opening
in the Kūpaianaha shield (USGS photo by J. D. Griggs,
1/13/87).

Figure 129. Channel-fed ʻaʻā flows emerging from the side of the Kūpaianaha shield, Puʻu ʻŌʻō-Kūpaianaha eruption. The open channels (*orange*) are about 6 to 10 feet (2–3 meters) wide and 6 feet (2 meters) deep; flow fronts are about 10 to 12 feet (3–4 meters) high. Lava in the channel moves at speeds up to 5 miles (8 kilometers) per hour, but the expanding flow front advances much more slowly (USGS photo by J. D. Griggs, 2/15/90).

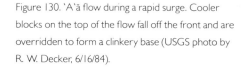

Figure 130. ʻAʻā flow during a rapid surge. Cooler blocks on the top of the flow fall off the front and are overridden to form a clinkery base (USGS photo by R. W. Decker, 6/16/84).

Figure 131. Front of an 'a'ā flow. The molten interior
of the flow shows as an intense yellow in the center of
the photo. Orange areas are cooler, grading outward
into black clinkers (USGS photo by J. Dvorak, 4/8/83).

Figure 132. Mauna Loa eruption of 1984. **A**, lava fountains during the "curtain of fire" phase marking the beginning of eruption (USGS photo by R. B. Moore, 3/25/84). **B**, ‘a‘ā channel as it appeared about a week after the eruption began. The increasing viscosity of the cooling crust, combined with cool blocks loosened from the channel walls, blocked the channel, causing an overflow and formation of a new ‘a‘ā channel (Lipman and Banks, 1987) (USGS photo by J. D. Griggs, 4/2/84).

132B.

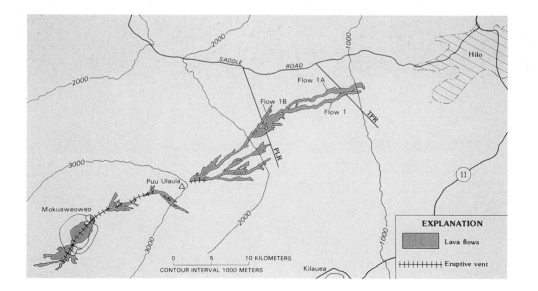

Figure 133. Natural lava diversion during the 1984 eruption of Mauna Loa. Flow *1* reached its terminus, about 4 miles (7 kilometers) from the outskirts of Hilo, in six days. The channel became blocked, ending the forward movement of flow *1* and beginning flow *1A*, which reached the same altitude as flow *1* over the next four days. Again, the channel was blocked and flow *1B* did not get as far downslope because the eruption was already waning by that time (Lipman and Banks, 1987, p. 1528).

THE CHALLENGE OF LIVING WITH AN ACTIVE VOLCANO

The Puʻu ʻŌʻō-Kūpaianaha eruption of Kīlauea, as of 1991 in its ninth year, is the most destructive eruption in Kīlauea's recent history (Heliker and Wright, 1991). During June 1989, the national park lost its visitor center at Wahaʻula (fig. 134). The same lava covered or threatened many archaeological sites, the most important surviving example of which is the Wahaʻula heiau, on higher ground behind the visitor center (fig. 135). The heiau is surrounded on three sides by new lava, piled higher than its walls.

In 1990 the paths of flows shifted to the eastern side of the lava field, where an ever-widening flow moved through the more recently developed parts of Kalapana, directed inland along the Hakuma pali (fig. 136) in its advance to the ocean. By the end of October of that year, lava flows destroyed all of Kalapana and filled in Kaimū Bay (fig. 137). At its most easterly point, lava covered much of the famous Kaimū black sand beach, but spared the community of Kaimū. A new black sand beach formed at Kaimū, a large lava delta replaced the former Kalapana surfing area, and lava built a small bench in front of Hakuma Point. During eight years of eruption — from 1983 to 1991 — more than 170 structures were destroyed by lava, and more than 280 acres (over one square kilometer) of new land were added to the island of Hawaiʻi (fig. 138). Dozens of structures unaffected by lava were damaged by an earthquake (June 25, 1989; magnitude 6.2) that relieved some of the strain built up by unerupted magma from the ongoing eruption pressing against Kīlauea's south flank.

Two striking statistics define a historical context for the activity at Kīlauea. Within the time of Hawaiian habitation —

about 1,500 years—more than 90 percent of the land surface of Kīlauea (fig. 139) has been covered by lava. The present caldera and many of the main features of the rift zones and fault systems have been formed or modified within that time. For Hawaiians, the loss of temples, such as Wahaʻula, or villages, such as Kealakomo, could not have been a rare event. An even more striking statistic underscores the recent and future hazard from Kīlauea's eruptions. Over the 32-mile stretch of Puna coastline traversed by Ellis (fig. 140), almost 30 percent of the land surface between the east rift zone and the ocean was covered by lava between 1955 and 1991 — less than half a century, and well within one person's lifetime. This area is still being developed (fig. 141), and, like the ancient Hawaiians, the present residents live in a lush, subtropical paradise, knowing that their land could be reclaimed (fig. 142) by an eruption of the volcano that created the paradise.

134A.

134B.

Figure 134. The demise of the Wahaʻula Visitor Center, Hawaii Volcanoes National Park. **A**, visitor center in use (USGS photo by T. J. Takahashi, 2/87). **B**, after destruction by lava in June 1989 (USGS photo by J. D. Griggs, 10/12/89).

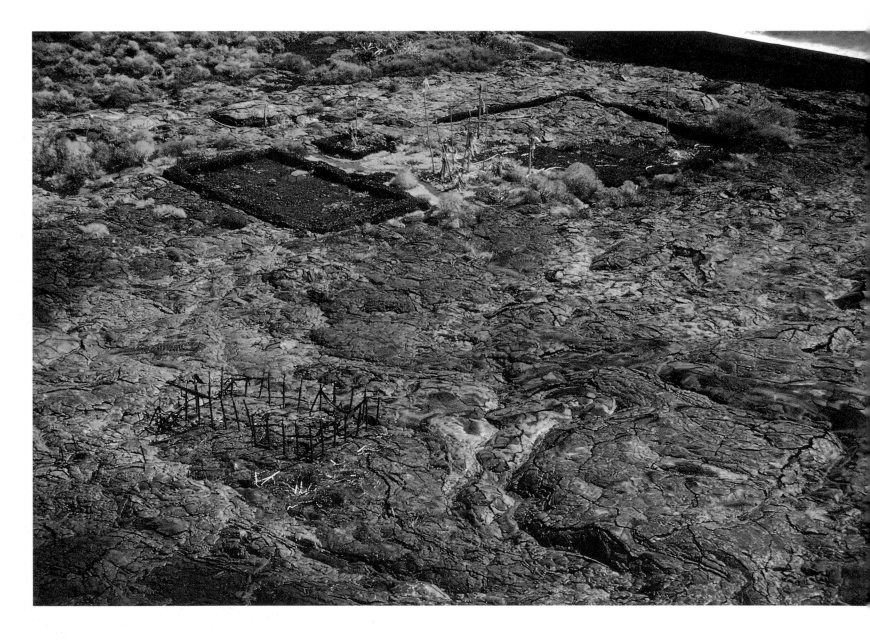

Figure 135. Aerial view of Wahaʻula heiau (*top center*), now surrounded by lava, and the remains of the Wahaʻula Visitor Center (*lower left*) (USGS photo by J. D. Griggs, 12/27/89).

Figure 136. Lava moving through Kalapana Gardens subdivision. The fault scarp (Hakuma pali) shown on the left side of the photo stood about 50 feet (15 meters) above the ground surface and directed the lava through the subdivision toward the ocean at Hakuma Point (*left foreground*). The older Kalapana village occupies the right foreground. Within the village the Mauna Kea Congregational Church is clearly visible, surrounded by open land (USGS photo by J. D. Griggs, 5/16/90).

137A.

Figure 137. The destruction of Kalapana and the filling of Kaimū Bay, April–October 1990. **A**, initial entry of lava into the Kalapana Gardens subdivision (*left center*) was in December 1986 (USGS photo by J. D. Griggs, 4/24/87). **B**, after destruction of much of Kalapana Gardens (photo by Air Survey Hawaii, 5/2/90). **C**, following destruction of the older part of Kalapana (USGS photo by D. Weisel, 8/20/90). **D**, after the filling of Kaimū Bay (USGS photo by D. Weisel, 12/7/90). **E**, oblique aerial view of the lava field following the filling of Kaimū Bay (USGS photo by J. D. Griggs, 10/31/90).

137B.

137C.

137D.

137E.

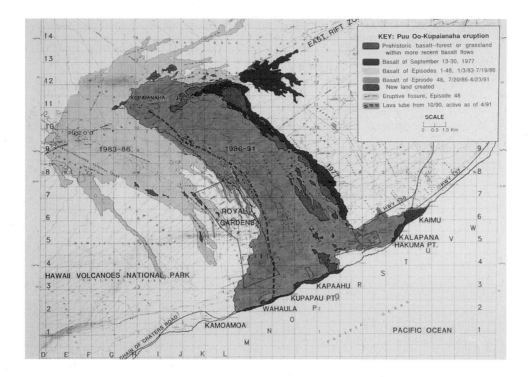

Figure 138. One in a series of working maps showing lava coverage during the Pu'u 'Ō'ō-Kūpaianaha eruption. Developed areas partially or entirely covered by lava include Royal Gardens, Kapa'ahu, and Kalapana. The lava tube, active at the time the map was prepared, was formed following the inundation of Kalapana (fig. 137). Lava tubes transporting lava toward Kalapana in 1990 were directed downslope, west of the steep border of the 1977 'a'ā flow. Once lava flows reached Highway 130, they were directed eastward by the Hakuma fault scarp, defined in this map by the flow boundary extending west from Hakuma Point. These two natural barriers virtually ensured the destruction of Kalapana (USGS map by C. C. Heliker and T. Mattox, 4/91).

Figure 139. Outline map of the five volcanoes that make up the island of Hawai'i. Over 90 percent of the land surface of Kīlauea (red) has been covered by lava since the arrival of the Hawaiians (USGS map).

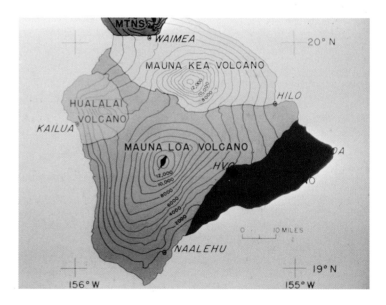

140A.

Figure 140. Southeast coast of Hawai'i traversed by Ellis. **A**, oblique aerial view taken from 1 mile (1.6 kilometers) from shore shows lava entering the ocean near Waha'ula (*steam plume, left skyline*) and the lighthouse at Cape Kumukahi (*extreme right foreground*). The east rift zone, marked by cinder cones, extends from Pu'u 'Ō'ō (steam plume, center skyline) to the right of, and behind, the lighthouse. Much of the area between the rift zone and the ocean is being developed for residential use (USGS photo by J. D. Griggs, 12/27/89). **B**, distribution of historical lava flows originating from Kīlauea's east rift zone. Approximately 29 percent of the coastline traversed by Ellis has been covered by lava since 1840 (computer-assisted drawing adapted from USGS base maps). For comparison with what Ellis saw, see Figure 15.

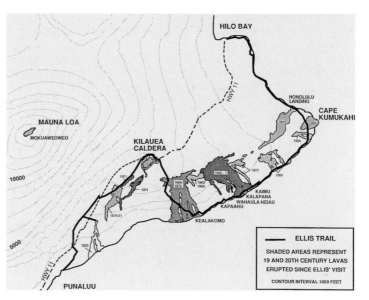

140B.

Figure 141. Home in Kalapana Gardens later
destroyed by lava (USGS photo by J. D. Griggs,
4/29/90).

Figure 142. Kalapana as it appeared when lava first threatened in December 1986 (USGS photo by J. D. Griggs, 12/19/86).

Epilogue

Eruptions and earthquakes will continue to play an important role in the lives of the residents of Hawai'i, particularly those who live on the island of Hawai'i. Millions of visitors to the islands have also been affected by the magnificent scenery created by volcanic activity and, for those fortunate enough to arrive during an eruption, by the manifest power of natural Earth forces. Visitors and residents alike can only benefit from living in harmony with nature, respecting, as did the Hawaiians, volcanic forces as essential for re-creation and perpetuation of our land. It is toward such an appreciation that we have prepared this pictorial history.

143A.

Figure 143. Volcano watching in Hawai`i. **A**, Hawaiians viewing the Hilo flow, painting by Charles Furneaux, 1881 (courtesy of Bishop Museum). **B**, More than a century later, residents of the community of Kapa`ahu watch lava from the Pu`u `Ō`ō-Kūpaianaha eruption enter Queen's Bath. Believed to be used originally by Hawaiian royalty, it later became a popular local bathing spot (USGS photo by J. D. Griggs, 3/31/87).

143B.

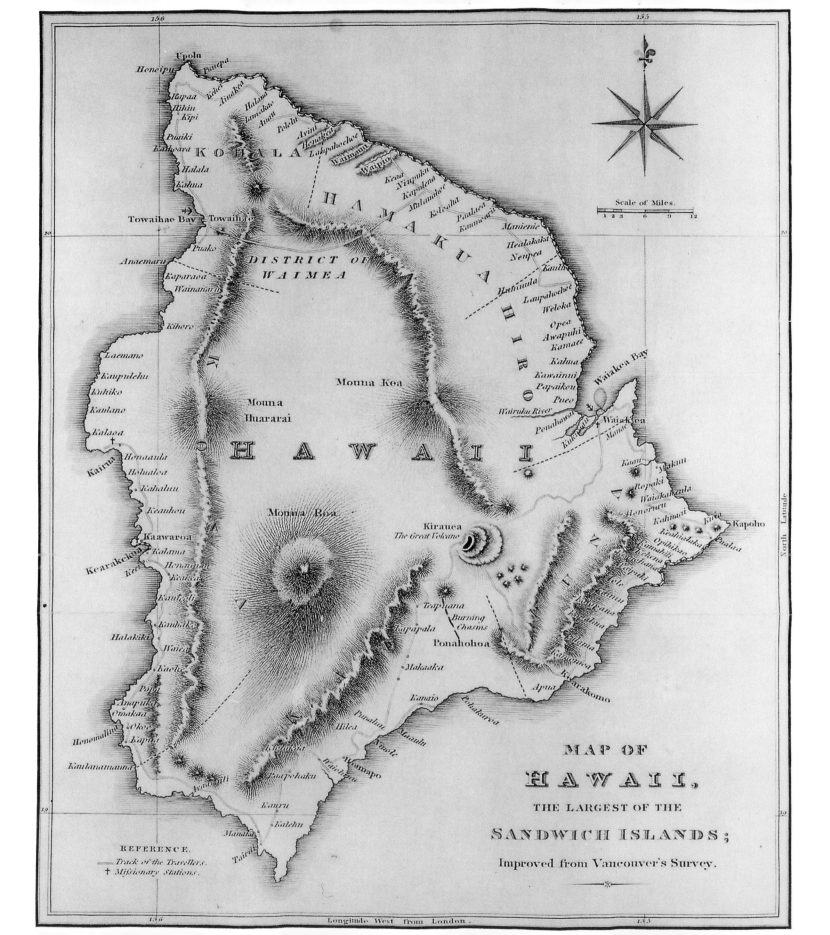

MAP OF
HAWAII,
THE LARGEST OF THE
SANDWICH ISLANDS;
Improved from Vancouver's Survey.

REFERENCE.
—— Track of the Travellers.
† Missionary Stations.

Longitude West from London.

APPENDIX

Table 1. Historical Eruptions of Hawai'i's Active Volcanoes

DATE OF ERUPTION		DURATION (days)	ALTITUDE (meters)	LOCATION	DATE OF ERUPTION		DURATION (days)	ALTITUDE (meters)	LOCATION
Year	Month and Day				Year	Month and Day			
Haleakalā, Maui					1907	Jan. 9	<1	3,900	Moku'āweoweo
ca. 1790	–	short	170; 465	SW rift zone	1907	Jan. 9	15	1,860	SW rift zone
					1914	Nov. 25	48	3,900	Moku'āweoweo
Hualālai					**1916**	May 19	12	2,220	SW rift zone
1800	–	–	1,650–1,800	NW rift zone	1919	Sept. 29	<1	3,900	Moku'āweoweo
1801	–	–	500	NW rift zone	**1919**	Sept. 29	38	2,310	SW rift zone
					1926	Apr. 10	<1	3,900	Moku'āweoweo
Mauna Loa					**1926**	Apr. 10	14	2,280	SW rift zone
1832	June 20	21	3,900	Moku'āweoweo	**1933**	Dec. 2	17	3,900	Moku'āweoweo
1843	Jan. 10	5	3,900	Moku'āweoweo	1935	Nov. 21	6	3,900	Moku'āweoweo
1843	Jan. 15	90	2,900	N flank	**1935–1936**	Nov. 27	40	3,630	NE rift zone
1849	May	15	3,900	Moku'āweoweo	1940	Apr. 17	134	3,900	Moku'āweoweo
1851	Aug. 8	21	3,900	Moku'āweoweo	1942	Apr. 26	2	3,900	Moku'āweoweo
1852	Feb. 17	1	3,900	Moku'āweoweo	1942	Apr. 28	13	2,760	NE rift zone
1852	Feb. 18	20	2,520	NE rift zone	1949	Jan. 6	145	3,900	Moku'āweoweo
1855	Aug. 11	<1	3,900	Moku'āweoweo	1950	June 1	1	3,900	Moku'āweoweo
1855–1856	Aug. 11	450	3,150 (?)	NE rift zone	**1950**	June 1	23	2,400	SW rift zone
1859	Jan. 23	<1	3,900	Moku'āweoweo	1975	July 5	1	3,900	Moku'āweoweo
1859	Jan. 23	300	2,760	N flank	1984	Mar. 26	<1	3,900	Moku'āweoweo
1865	Dec. 30	120	3,900	Moku'āweoweo	**1984**	Mar. 26	22	2,900	NE rift zone
1868	Mar. 27	1	3,900	Moku'āweoweo					
1868	Mar. 27	15	990	SW rift zone					
1871	Aug. 10	20	3,900	Moku'āweoweo	**Kīlauea**				
1872–1875	Aug. 9 (Nearly continuous eruption)	1,200	3,900	Moku'āweoweo	1750 (?)	–	–	510	E rift zone
1876	Feb. 13	Short	3,900	Moku'āweoweo	1790 (?)	–	–	330–250	E rift zone
1877	Feb. 14	<1	3,900	Moku'āweoweo	**1790**	Nov. (Series of explosive eruptions)		1,110	Kīlauea caldera
1877	Feb. 14	<1	–55 ±	W flank	**1823–1894**	Continuous lava lake			Kīlauea caldera
1880	May 1	6	3,900	Moku'āweoweo	**1823**	Feb.-July	Short	510–250	SW rift zone
1880–1881	Nov. 5	280	3,120	NE rift zone	**1832**	Jan. 14	Short	1,110	Byron's Ledge
1887	Jan. 16	<1	3,900	Moku'āweoweo	**1840**	May 30	26	930–250	E rift zone
1887	Jan. 16	7	1,710	SW rift zone	**1868**	Apr. 2	Short	1,110	Kīlauea Iki
1892	Nov. 30	3	3,900	Moku'āweoweo	**1868**	Apr. 2	Short	770	SW rift zone
1896	Apr. 21	16	3,900	Moku'āweoweo	1877	May 4	Short	1,110	Keanakāko'i
1899	July 1	4	3,900	Moku'āweoweo	1885	Mar.	~80	1,110	Kīlauea caldera
1899	July 5	21	3,210	NE rift zone	**1894**	Mar. 21	~6	1,110	Kīlauea caldera
1903	Oct. 6	60	3,900	Moku'āweoweo	1894–1907	Intermittent lava lake			Halema'uma'u

Table 1. Historical Eruptions of Hawai'i's Active Volcanoes (continued)

Year	Month and Day	Duration (days)	Altitude (meters)	Location
1907–1924	Continuous lava lake			Halema'uma'u
1918	Feb. 23	14	1,110	Kīlauea caldera
1919	Feb. 7	294	1,110	Kīlauea caldera
1919–1920	Dec. 21	221	900	SW rift zone
1921	Mar. 18	7	1,110	Kīlauea caldera
1922	May 28	2	800–720	E rift zone
1923	Aug. 25	1	900	E rift zone
1924	May 10	17	1,110	Halema'uma'u
	(Phreatic explosions; end of continuous lava lake)			
1924	July 19	11	710	Halema'uma'u
1927	July 7	13	720	Halema'uma'u
1929	Feb. 20	2	750	Halema'uma'u
1929	July 25	4	770	Halema'uma'u
1930	Nov. 19	19	780	Halema'uma'u
1931–1932	Dec. 23	14	810	Halema'uma'u
1934	Sept. 6	33	840	Halema'uma'u
1952	June 27	136	860	Halema'uma'u
1954	May 31	3	950–1,110	Halema'uma'u and Kīlauea caldera
1955	Feb. 28	88	390–50	E rift zone
1959	Nov. 14	36	1,110	Kīlauea Iki
1960	Jan. 13	36	35	E rift zone
1961	Feb. 24	1	940	Halema'uma'u
1961	Mar. 3	22	940	Halema'uma'u
1961	July 10	7	940	Halema'uma'u
1961	Sept. 22	3	780–390	E rift zone
1962	Dec. 7	2	980–930	E rift zone
1963	Aug. 21	2	940–810	E rift zone
1963	Oct. 5	1	830–690	E rift zone
1965	Mar. 5	10	900–690	E rift zone
1965	Dec. 24	<1	940–900	E rift zone
1967–1968	Nov. 5	251	940	Halema'uma'u
1968	Aug. 22	5	870–570	E rift zone
1968	Oct. 7	15	900–720	E rift zone
1969	Feb. 22	6	930–870	E rift zone
1969–1971	May 24	867	940	E rift zone
1971	Aug. 14	<1	1,110–1,080	Kīlauea caldera
1971	Sept. 24	5	1,110–820	Kīlauea caldera and upper SW rift zone
1972–1974	Feb.4	455	940	E rift zone
1973	May 5	<1	1,000–980	E rift zone
1973	Nov. 10	30	980–870	E rift zone
1973	Dec. 12	203	940	E rift zone
1974	July 19	3	1,110–980	Kīlauea caldera and upper E rift zone
1974	Sept. 19	<1	1,100	Kīlauea caldera
1974	Dec. 31	<1	1,080	SW rift zone
1975	Nov. 29	<1	1,080–1,060	Kīlauea caldera
1977	Sept. 13	18	620–480	E rift zone
1979	Nov. 16	1	980–960	E rift zone
1982	Apr. 31	<1	1,110	Kīlauea caldera
1982	Sept. 25	<1	1,110	Kīlauea caldera
1983	Jan. 3	>3,200	630–800	E rift zone

Source: Macdonald et al., 1983; Mauna Loa data corrected and recompiled by Lockwood and Lipman, 1987.

Note: **Boldface** refers to eruptions mentioned in text.

Table 2. Firsthand Accounts of Eruptions in Hawai'i, 1790–1924

Date	Eruption	Observer	Primary Reference(s)
pre-1790	Kīlauea	Hawaiian	Hitchcock, WT 708
1790 (?)	Haleakalā	Hawaiian	Thurston, WT 1170
1790	Kīlauea summit	Hawaiian	Dibble, WT 530; Ellis, WT 561
1800–1801	Hualālai	Hawaiian	Ellis, WT 561
1823–1894	Kīlauea summit	Missionary, scientist, lay person, artist	Brigham, WT 306; Dana, WT 485, 486, 488; Hitchcock, WT 708; Volcano House Register, WT 261
1823	Kīlauea SW rift zone	Hawaiian	Ellis, WT 561
1832	Kīlauea summit	Missionary	Dibble, WT 530; Goodrich, WT 637
1832	Mauna Loa summit	Missionary	Goodrich, WT 637
1840	Kīlauea E rift zone	Hawaiian	Coan, WT 367; Wilkes, WT 1259
1843	Mauna Loa N flank	Missionary	Coan, WT 368, 369
1851	Mauna Loa summit	Missionary	Coan, WT 372
1852	Mauna Loa NE rift zone	Missionary	Coan, WT 373; Fuller, WT 627; Kinney, WT 858
1855–1856	Mauna Loa NE rift zone	Missionary	Coan, WT 382–388; Weld, WT 1220
1859	Mauna Loa N flank	Lay person, missionary, scientist	Alexander, WT 7; Green, WT 646; Haskell, WT 673–675; Whitney, WT 1244
1865–1866	Mauna Loa summit	Missionary	Coan, WT 395
1868	Kīlauea summit	Missionary, lay person	Coan, WT 401–402; Hillebrand, WT 693; Whitney, WT 1248
1868	Kīlauea SW rift zone	Missionary	Coan, WT 402
1868	Mauna Loa SW rift zone, earthquakes	Missionary, lay person	Brigham, WT 295; Coan, WT 398–402; Fornander, WT 609; Lyman, WT 887–888; Whitney, WT 1246–1248
1870–1875	Mauna Loa summit	Missionary, lay person	Bird, WT 265; Coan, WT 404–410; Green, WT 652
1877	Mauna Loa, Kealakekua Bay	Lay person	Mist, WT 970; Whitney, WT 1250
1880–1881	Mauna Loa NE rift zone	Missionary, lay person, artist	Barton, WT 247; Coan, WT 413–418; Emerson, WT 569; Gordon-Cumming, WT 641; Hall, WT 670; Hitchcock, WT 713–714; Oleson, WT 988
1887	Mauna Loa SW rift zone	Missionary, lay person	Bishop, WT 268–270; Jones, WT 846–847; Maby, WT 905; Martin, WT 951; Paris, WT 1002; Spencer, WT 1114
1894	Kīlauea summit	Lay person, artist	Thurston, WT 1163; Volcano House Register, WT 261
1896	Mauna Loa summit	Scientist, artist	Dodge, WT 540; Friedlaender, WT 617–618
1894–1907	Kīlauea summit, intermittent	Lay person	Volcano House Register, WT 261
1899	Mauna Loa NE rift zone	Missionary, lay person	Castle, WT 342; Wood, WT 1279
1903	Mauna Loa summit	Lay person	Thrum, WT 1161; Wood, WT 1280; newspaper accounts
1907	Mauna Loa SW rift zone	Missionary, lay person	Baker, WT 215; Bishop, WT 275; McDougall, WT 956; newspaper accounts
1907–1924	Kīlauea summit	Scientist, lay person	HVO Early Serial Reports, WT 262; Volcano House Register, WT 261
1916, 1919	Mauna Loa SW rift zone	Scientist, lay person	HVO Early Serial Reports, WT 262; Volcano House Register, WT 261
1922	Kīlauea E rift zone	Scientist, lay person	HVO Early Serial Reports, WT 262; Volcano House Register, WT 261
1923	Kīlauea E rift zone	Scientist, lay person	HVO Early Serial Reports, WT 262; Volcano House Register, WT 261
1924	Kīlauea summit, E rift zone (earthquakes)	Scientist	Finch, WT 582–584; HVO Early Serial Reports, WT 262; Stearns, WT 1118

BIBLIOGRAPHY

Note: Citations in the text and figure captions are to author and date. Many of these references have been annotated in Wright and Takahashi 1989, in which case we give the number of the annotated reference at the end of the citation; for example, [WT 291] refers to reference 291 in Wright and Takahashi, 1989.

Albright, H. M. [as told to R. Cahn]. 1985. The birth of the National Park Service: the founding years, 1913–33. In A. M. Josephy, Jr., ed., *Institute of the American West books,* vol. 2. Salt Lake City: Howe Brothers, 335 pp.

Alexander, W. D. 1859. Later details from the volcano on Hawaii. *Pacific Commercial Advertiser,* Feb. 24, p. 2. [WT 7]

Anderson, B. 1960. *Surveyor of the sea: the life and voyages of Captain George Vancouver.* Seattle: University of Washington Press, 274 pp.

Anonymous. 1929. Eruption of Hualalai predicted by Jaggar. *New York Times,* Sept. 27. [WT 197]

Apple, R. A. 1987. Thomas A. Jaggar and the Hawaiian Volcano Observatory. In R. W. Decker, T. L. Wright, and P. H. Stauffer, eds., *Volcanism in Hawaii.* 2 vols. U.S. Geological Survey Professional Paper 1350, vol. 2, pp. 1619–1644. [WT 206]

Appleman, D. E. 1987. James D. Dana and the origins of Hawaiian volcanology: the U.S. Exploring Expedition in Hawaii, 1840–41. In R. W. Decker, T. L. Wright, and P. H. Stauffer, eds., *Volcanism in Hawaii.* 2 vols. U.S. Geological Survey Professional Paper 1350, vol. 2, p. 1607–1618. [WT 207]

Baker, E. P. 1885. The ascent of Mauna Loa. *Hawaiian Gazette,* May 27, p. 4. [WT 218]

Barnard, W. M. ed. 1990. *Mauna Loa—a source book: historical eruption and exploration.* Vol. 1, *From 1778 through 1907.* Fredonia, N.Y.: W. M. Barnard. 353 pp.

Barr, P. 1970. *A curious life for a lady: the story of Isabella Bird.* Garden City: Doubleday & Co., 347 pp.

Bevens, D., transcriber. 1988. *Volcano House register,* 1865–1955. Unpublished record, Hawaii Natural History Association. 10 vols., with supp. of newspaper clippings. [*See* Hitchcock, 1909, p. 205.] [WT 261]

Bevens, D., compiler. 1992. *On the rim of Kilauea: excerpts from the Volcano House register.* Hawaii National Park: Hawaii Natural History Association.

Bevens, D., T. J. Takahashi, and T. L. Wright, eds. 1988. *The early serial publications of the Hawaiian Volcano Observatory.* 3 vols. Hawaii National Park, Hawaii Natural History Association, vol. 1, 565 pp.; vol. 2, 1273 pp.; vol. 3, 1224 pp. [WT 262]

Bird, I. L. [I. L. Bishop]. 1875. *Six months among the palm groves, coral reefs and volcanoes of the Sandwich Islands.* London: John Murray & Sons [reprinted 1882, 1890; 1974 by Charles E. Tuttle Co., Rutland, Vt.; 1964, 1966 by University of Hawaii Press, Honolulu, 278 pp.].

Brigham, W. T. 1868. Notes on the volcanic phenomena of the Hawaiian Islands, with a description of the modern eruptions. *Boston Society of Natural History Memoirs,* vol. 1, pt. 3, pp. 341–372 [reprinted 1968 by Riverside Press, Cambridge, 132 pp.; includes maps]. [WT 294]

_____. 1909. *The volcanoes of Kilauea and Mauna Loa on the island of Hawaii.* Bernice P. Bishop Museum Memoirs, vol. 2, no. 4, 222 pp.; plates, 56 pp. [reprinted 1974 by Kraus Reprint Co., Millwood, N.Y.]. [WT 306]

Byron, G. (Lord). 1826. *Voyage of H.M.S.* Blonde *to the Sandwich Islands, in the years 1824–1825*. London: John Murray, pp. 169–191. [WT 333]

Clague, D. A., and G. B. Dalrymple. 1987. The Hawaiian-Emperor volcanic chain, pt. I: geologic evolution. In R. W. Decker, T. L. Wright, and P. H. Stauffer, eds., *Volcanism in Hawaii*. 2 vols. U.S. Geological Survey Professional Paper 1350, vol. 1: 5–54.

Coan, F. C. 1852. Eruption from the summit of Mauna Loa, Hawaii. *American Journal of Science,* 2d ser., 14: 106–107. [WT 363]

Coan, L. B. 1881. [On the 1881 lava flow of Mauna Loa]. *Hawaiian Gazette,* July 6, p. 3. [WT 364]

——————. 1884. *Titus Coan: a memorial*. Chicago: Fleming H. Revell, 248 pp. [WT 365]

Coan, T. 1856. On the eruption at Hawaii. *American Journal of Science,* 2d ser., 22: 240–243. [WT 384]

——————. 1869. Notes on the recent volcanic disturbances of Hawaii. *American Journal of Science,* 2d ser., 47: 89–98. [WT 402]

——————. 1880. Recent action of Mauna Loa and Kilauea. *American Journal of Science,* 3d ser., 20: 71–72. [WT 413]

——————. 1882. *Life in Hawaii*. New York: Anson D. F. Randolph & Co., 340 pp. [WT 418]

Coan, T. M. 1871. An island on fire. *Scribner's Monthly,* vol. 2, Oct., pp. 561–573. [WT 419]

Dana, J. D. 1849. *Geology: United States Exploring Expedition,* vol. 10. New York: George P. Putnam, 756 pp. [sections on Mauna Loa and Kilauea are reorganized and partly rewritten in *American Journal of Science,* 2d ser., 9 (1850): 347–364; 10 (1850): 235–244]. [WT 471]

——————. 1887. History of the changes in the Mt. Loa craters. *American Journal of Science,* 3rd ser., 33: 433–451; 34: 81–97, 349–364 [includes maps]. [WT 485]

——————. 1891. *Characteristics of volcanoes*. New York: Dodd, Mead, & Company, 399 pp. [WT 488]

Dibble, S. 1843. *A history of the Sandwich Islands*. Lahainaluna, T. H.: T. G. Thrum, 451 pp. [reprinted 1909 in Honolulu]. [WT 530]

Dutton, C. E. 1884. The Hawaiian volcanoes. In *U.S. Geological Survey, 4th Annual Report*. Washington, D. C.: Government Printing Office, pp. 75–219 [pp. 183–198 reprinted 1884 as "The volcanic problem stated" in Philosophical Society of Washington, *Bulletin* 6 (1884): 87–92; also reprinted in *Hawaiian Monthly,* vol. 1, no. 9 (1884): 193–200]. [WT 557]

Dynamic Graphics. 1984. *The Hawaiian Islands*. Berkeley, Calif.: Dynamic Graphics, Inc. [computer-drawn perspective model of the ocean floor around the Hawaiian Islands, bathymetric contour interval 1000 m, vertical exaggeration 6x].

Dzurisin, D., R. Y. Koyanagi, and T. T. English, 1984. Magma supply and storage at Kilauea Volcano, Hawaii, 1956–1983. *Journal of Volcanology and Geothermal Research* 21: 177–206.

Eaton, J. P., and K. J. Murata, 1960. How volcanoes grow. *Science* 132: 925–938.

Eaton, J. P., D. H. Richter, and H. L. Krivoy. 1987. Cycling of magma between the summit reservoir and Kilauea Iki lava lake during the 1959 eruption of Kilauea Volcano. In R. W. Decker, T. L. Wright, and P. H. Stauffer, eds.,

Volcanism in Hawaii. 2 vols. U.S. Geological Survey Professional Paper 1350, vol. 2, pp. 1307–1335.

Ellis, W. 1825. *Narrative of a tour through Hawaii, or, Owhyhee*. London: H. Fisher, Son, & P. Jackson [reprinted 1826, 1827; reprinted 1917 by Hawaiian Gazette Co., Ltd., Honolulu; 1827 London ed. was reprinted 1963 as *Journal of William Ellis* by the Advertiser Publishing Co., Ltd., Honolulu, 342 pp.]. [WT 561]

Emory, K. P., E. J. Ladd, and L. J. Soehren. 1965. *The archeological resources of Hawaii Volcanoes National Park, Hawaii, pt. II. Additional sites, test observations, and petroglyphs*. Honolulu, Bernice P. Bishop Museum, Department of Anthropology, 44 pp.; plates, 3 pp.

Finch, R. H., and G. A. Macdonald. 1953. *Hawaiian volcanoes during 1950*. U.S. Geological Survey Bulletin 996-B, pp. 27–89. [WT 595]

Fiske, R.S., T. Simkin, and E. A. Nielsen, eds. 1987. *The Volcano Letter*. Washington, D. C.: Smithsonian Institution Press, 539 pp. [compiled and reprinted; originally published 1925–1955 by the Hawaiian Volcano Observatory]. [WT 597]

Fitzpatrick, G. L. 1986. *The early mapping of Hawaii*. Honolulu: Editions Limited, vol. 1, 160 pp. [WT 598]

Fornari, D. J., M. O. Garcia, R. C. Tyce, and D. G. Gallo. 1988. Morphology and structure of Loihi Seamount based on SEA BEAM sonar mapping. *Journal of Geophysical Research,* vol. 93, no. B12: 15,227–15,238 (plate 1, p. 14,359).

Gordon-Cumming, C. F. 1883. *Fire fountains*. Vol. 2. Edinburgh: William Blackwood and Sons, 279 pp.

Guppy, H. B. 1897. On the summit of Mauna Loa. *Pacific Commercial Advertiser,* Sept. 18, pp. 1, 5 [also excerpted and published as "Three weeks camp at Mokuaweoweo" in *The Friend,* Oct., 1897, p. 82]. [WT 664]

Hawaiian Mission Children's Society. 1969. *The missionary album*. Honolulu: Hawaiian Mission Children's Society, 222 pp.

Heezen, B. C., and M. Tharp. 1977. *World ocean floor*. Washington, D. C.: United States Navy, Office of Naval Research [map, scale 1:30,000,000].

Heliker, C. C., and T. L. Wright. 1991. The Pu'u O'o-Kupaianaha eruption of Kīlauea: *Eos* 72: 521, 526, 530.

Heliker, C. C., J. D. Griggs, T. J. Takahashi, and T. L. Wright. 1986. Volcano monitoring at the U.S. Geological Survey's Hawaiian Volcano Observatory. *Earthquakes and Volcanoes,* vol. 18, no. 1, 71 pp.

Herbert, D., and F. Bardossi. 1968. *Kilauea: case history of a volcano*. New York: Harper & Row, 191 pp.

Hitchcock, C. H. 1909. *Hawaii and its volcanoes*. Honolulu: Hawaiian Gazette Co., 314 pp.; 2d ed., with supp., 1911, 314 pp.

Honolulu Advertiser. 1955. Second volcano pictorial section on the 1955 Puna eruption. *Honolulu Advertiser,* Mar. 27, pp. A1, D1.

Jackson, F. 1966. *National parks in Hawaii, 50 years: 1916–1966; a short history of Hawaii Volcanoes National Park and Haleakala National Park*. Hawaii National Park: Hawaii Natural History Association, 60 pp.

Jaggar, T. A. 1912. The cross of Hawaii. Honolulu Chamber of Commerce, Annual Report, 12 pp. [reprinted in Mid-Pacific Magazine, vol. 7, June 1914, pp. 552–557]. [WT 743]

_____. 1913. *Scientific work on Hawaiian volcanoes*. Special Bulletin of the Hawaiian Volcano Observatory. [See Bevens and others, 1988, vol. 1, pp. 478–492.] [WT 262]

_____. 1916. *A bill [H.R. 9525] to establish a national park in the Territory of Hawaii; hearing before the committee on public lands, Feb. 3, 1916*. Washington, D. C.: Government Printing Office, pp. 330. [WT 752]

_____. 1925. Submarine landscape off Hawaii. *The Volcano Letter*, no. 49. [See Fiske and others, 1987.] [WT 597]

_____. 1929. Seismic crisis on Hawaii. *The Volcano Letter*, no. 248. [See Fiske and others, 1987.] [WT 597]

_____. 1931. The crater of Mauna Loa. *The Volcano Letter*, no. 360. [See Fiske and others, 1987.] [WT 597]

_____. 1934. The new outbreak of Kilauea, 1934. *Paradise of the Pacific*, vol. 46, Oct., pp. 5–11.

_____. 1936a. The coming lava flow. *The Volcano Letter*, no. 440, pp. 1–6. [See Fiske and others, 1987.] [WT 597]

_____. 1936b. The bombing of Mauna Loa, 1935. *The Volcano Letter*, no. 442, pp. 1–7. [See Fiske and others, 1987.] [WT 597]

_____. 1937. Protection of Hilo from coming lava flows. *The Volcano Letter*, no. 443, pp. 1–8. [See Fiske and others, 1987.] [WT 597]

_____. 1945a. *Volcanoes declare war*. Honolulu: Paradise of the Pacific, 166 pp. [WT 811]

_____. 1945b. *The vision of deep sea science*. N. p. [Pamphlet.] [WT 813]

Judd, G. P. 1911. *The letters of Dr. Gerrit P. Judd, 1827–1872*. Honolulu: Paradise of the Pacific, 239 pp. [WT 848]

Kinoshita, W. T., R. Y. Koyanagi, T. L. Wright, and R. S. Fiske. 1969. Kilauea Volcano: the 1967–1968 summit eruption. *Science* 166: 459–468.

Krukenberg, C. F. 1877. *Mikrographie der Glasbasalte von Hawaii*. Tübingen: Heinrich Laupp, 38 pp.; plates, 4 pp. [reviewed by C. F. Mohr, in *Niederrheinische Gessellschaft fur Naturund Heilunnde*. Bonn: Sitzungsberichte, no. 34, pp. 213–219]. [WT 864]

Ledyard, J. 1783. *A journal of Captain Cook's last voyage to the Pacific Ocean and in quest of a northwest passage between Asia and America*. Hartford, Conn.: Nathaniel Patten [published 1963 as J. K. Munford, ed., *John Ledyard's Journal of Captain Cook's Last Voyage*. Corvallis: Oregon State University Press, 265 pp.]. [WT 871]

Lipman, P. W., and N. G. Banks. 1987. Aa flow dynamics, Mauna Loa 1984. In R.W. Decker, T. L. Wright, and P. H. Stauffer, eds., *Volcanism in Hawaii*. 2 vols. U.S. Geological Survey Professional Paper 1350, vol. 2, pp. 1527–1567.

Lockwood, J. P., and P. W. Lipman. 1980. Recovery of datable charcoal from beneath young lavas—lessons from Hawaii. *Bulletin Volcanologique* 43: 609–615.

Lockwood, J. P., N. G. Banks, T. T. English, L. P. Greenland, D. B. Jackson, R. Y. Koyanagi, K. A. McGee, A. T. Okamura, and J. M. Rhodes. 1985. The 1984 eruption of Mauna Loa Volcano, Hawaii. *Eos* 66: 169–171.

Logan, D. 1903. *Hawaiian volcanoes*. Honolulu: n.p., 24 pp. [WT 879]

Lyman, C. S. 1851. On the recent condition of Kilauea. *American Journal of Science*, 2d ser., 12: 75–80. [WT 884]

Macdonald, G. A. 1955. *Hawaiian volcanoes during 1952*. U.S. Geological Survey Bulletin 1021-B, pp. 15–108 [includes plates]. [WT 929]

_____. 1962. The 1955 and 1960 eruptions of Kilauea Volcano, Hawaii, and the construction of walls to restrict the spread of the lava flows. *Bulletin Volcanologique* 24: 249–294.

Macdonald, G. A., and J. P. Eaton. 1964. *Hawaiian volcanoes during 1955*. U.S. Geological Survey Bulletin 1171, 170 pp. [includes plates]. [WT 933]

Macdonald, G. A., A. T. Abbott, and F. L. Peterson. 1983. *Volcanoes in the sea*. Honolulu: University of Hawaii Press, 517 pp.

Maxon, H. H. 1987. *D. Howard Hitchcock, islander*. Honolulu: Topgallant Publishing Co., 226 pp.

Mitchell, H. C. 1930. *Triangulation in Hawaii*. U.S. Coast and Geodetic Survey. Special Publication no. 156, 219 pp. [includes maps]. [WT 971]

Moore, J. G., D. A. Clague, R. T. Holcomb, P. W. Lipman, W. R. Normark, and M. E. Torresan. 1989. Prodigious submarine landslides on the Hawaiian Ridge. *Journal of Geophysical Research* 94: 17, 465–17,484.

Olson, G. E. 1941. *The story of the Volcano House*. Hilo: Petroglyph Press, 93 pp. [reprinted 1974].

Oostdam, B. L. 1965. Age of lava flows on Haleakala, Maui, Hawaii. *Geological Society of America Bulletin* 76: 393–394.

Paradise of the Pacific. 1926. [Portrait of William Brigham.] *Paradise of the Pacific*, vol. 39, no. 3.

Peck, D. L., T. L. Wright, and R. W. Decker. 1979. The lava lakes of Kilauea. *Scientific American* 241: 114–128.

Perret, F. A. 1913a. The circulatory system in the Halemaumau lava lake during the summer of 1911. *American Journal of Science*, 4th ser., 35: 337–349. [WT 1014]

_____. 1913b. Volcanic research at Kilauea in the summer of 1911. *American Journal of Science*, 4th ser., 36: 475–483. [WT 1018]

Rabbit, M. C. 1980. *Minerals, lands, and geology for the common defense and general welfare, vol. 2, 1879–1904, U.S. Geological Survey*. Washington, D.C.: Government Printing Office, 307 pp.

Rees, R. N. 1841. A late visit to the volcano of Kirauea, in Hawaii, one of the Sandwich Islands. *United Service Journal*, Aug., pp. 501–507 [reprinted in *Littell's Museum of Foreign Literature*, vol. 43, pp. 236–239]. [WT 1073]

Richter, D. H., J. P. Eaton, K. J. Murata, W. U. Ault, and H. L. Krivoy. 1970. Chronological narrative of the 1959–60 eruption of Kilauea Volcano, Hawaii. U.S. Geological Survey Professional Paper 537-E, 73 pp.

Shepherd, E. S. 1925. The analysis of gases obtained from volcanoes and from rocks. *Journal of Geology*, vol. 33 supp., pp. 289–370. [WT 1098]

Stearns, H. T. 1925. The explosive phase of Kilauea Volcano, Hawaii, in 1924. *Bulletin Volcanologique*, 2e ann., no. 5-6: pp. 193–208. [WT 1118]

_____. 1926. The Keaiwa or 1823 lava flow from Kilauea Volcano, Hawaii. *Journal of Geology* 34: 336–351. [WT 1122]

Stearns, H. T., and W. O. Clark. 1930. *Geology and water resources of the Kau District, Hawaii*. U.S. Geological Survey Water Supply Paper 616, 194 pp. [3 maps in pocket]. [WT 1134]

Stearns, H. T., and G. A. Macdonald. 1946. *Geology and ground-water resources of the Island of Hawaii.* Hawaii Division of Hydrography, Bulletin 9, 363 pp. [3 maps in pocket]. [WT 1135]

Swanson, D. A., and R. L. Christiansen. 1973. Tragic base surge in 1790 at Kilauea Volcano. *Geology* 1: 83–86. [WT 1151]

Swanson, D. A., W. A. Duffield, D. B. Jackson, and D. W. Peterson. 1979. Chronological narrative of the 1969–71 Mauna Ulu eruption of Kilauea Volcano, Hawaii. U.S. Geological Survey Professional Paper 1056, 55 pp.

Thurston, L. A. 1924. The last lava flow on Maui. *Honolulu Advertiser,* Feb. 24, pp. 9–10 [includes map]. [WT 1170]

Tilling, R. I., R. Y. Koyanagi, P. W. Lipman, J. P. Lockwood, J. G. Moore, and D. A. Swanson. 1976. *Earthquake and related catastrophic events, Island of Hawaii, November 29, 1975: a preliminary report.* U.S. Geological Survey Circular 740, pp. 1–33.

Tilling, R. I., R. L. Christiansen, W. A. Duffield, E. T. Endo, R. T. Holcomb, R. Y. Koyanagi, D. W. Peterson, and J. D. Unger. 1987. The 1972–1974 Mauna Ulu eruption, Kilauea Volcano. In R. W. Decker, T. L. Wright, and P. H. Stauffer, *Volcanism in Hawaii.* 2 vols. U.S. Geological Survey Professional Paper 1350, vol. 1, pp. 405–469.

Viola, H. J., and C. Margolis, eds. 1985. *Magnificent voyagers: the U.S. Exploring Expedition, 1834–1842.* Washington, D. C.: Smithsonian Institution Press, 304 pp.

Westerveldt, W. D. 1916. *Hawaiian legends of volcanoes.* Rutland, Vt.: Charles E. Tuttle Co., 210 pp. [reprinted 1963]. [WT 1240]

Wilkes, C. 1845. *Narrative of the U.S. Exploring Expedition during the years 1838–1842,* vol. 4. Philadelphia: Lee & Blanchard, pp. 87–231. [WT 1259]

Wilson, R. M. 1935. *Ground surface movements at Kilauea Volcano, Hawaii.* Honolulu: University of Hawaii Research Publication no. 10, 56 pp. [WT 1268]

Wolfe, E. W., M. O. Garcia, D. B. Jackson, R. Y. Koyanagi, and C. A. Neal. 1987. The Puu Oo eruption of Kilauea Volcano, episodes 1–20, January 3, 1983, to June 8, 1984. In R. W. Decker, T. L. Wright, and P. H. Stauffer, *Volcanism in Hawaii.* 2 vols. U.S. Geological Survey Professional Paper 1350, vol. 1, pp. 471–508.

Wolfe, E. W., and J. Morris, compilers. In preparation. Geologic map of the Island of Hawaii: U.S. Geological Survey.

Wright, T. L., and R. S. Fiske. 1971. Origin of the differentiated and hybrid lavas of Kilauea Volcano, Hawaii. *Journal of Petrology* 12: 1–65.

Wright, T. L., and T. J. Takahashi. 1989. *Observations and interpretation of Hawaiian volcanism and seismicity, 1779–1955: an annotated bibliography and subject index.* Honolulu: University of Hawaii Press, 270 pp.

Wyss, M., and R. Y. Koyanagi. 1992. *Isoseismal maps, macroseismic epicenters, and estimated magnitudes of historical earthquakes in the Hawaiian Islands.* U.S. Geological Survey Bulletin 2006, 91 pp.

Wyss, M., R. Y. Koyanagi, and D. C. Cox. 1992. *The Lyman Hawaiian earthquake diary.* U.S. Geological Survey Bulletin 2027, 34 pp.

INDEX